T0209321

The Kindergarten Run

Spirit Gives Guidance on Peace, Grief, Loss, and Healing. They Also Explain How the Other Side Works and Who Gets to Go There.

BOB JACOBS

BALBOA.PRESS
A DIVISION OF HAY HOUSE

Balboa Press books may be ordered through booksellers or by contacting:

Balboa Press
A Division of Hay House
1663 Liberty Drive
Bloomington, IN 47403
www.balboapress.com
1 (877) 407-4847

Because of the dynamic nature of the Internet, any web addresses or
links contained in this book may have changed since publication and
may no longer be valid. The views expressed in this work are solely those
of the author and do not necessarily reflect the views of the publisher,
and the publisher hereby disclaims any responsibility for them.

The author of this book does not dispense medical advice or prescribe the use
of any technique as a form of treatment for physical, emotional, or medical
problems without the advice of a physician, either directly or indirectly. The
intent of the author is only to offer information of a general nature to help
you in your quest for emotional and spiritual well-being. In the event you use
any of the information in this book for yourself, which is your constitutional
right, the author and the publisher assume no responsibility for your actions.

Any people depicted in stock imagery provided by Getty Images are
models, and such images are being used for illustrative purposes only.
Certain stock imagery © Getty Images.

Print information available on the last page.

ISBN: 978-1-9822-5021-8 (sc)
ISBN: 978-1-9822-5023-2 (hc)
ISBN: 978-1-9822-5022-5 (e)

Library of Congress Control Number: 2020911966

Balboa Press rev. date: 06/29/2020

I am grateful for the help I received in finishing this book.
Proofreading- Barb Jacobs and Sharon Gullett
Interior sketches and formatting – Jennifer Jacobs

CONTENTS

⊛ ⊛ ⊛

PART I
Peace, Spirit Guides, The Temple and Palace

PART II
Grief, Loss, Healing, and Signs

PART III
The Other Side

DEDICATION

●　●　●

I WROTE THE manuscript for this book during the Coronavirus outbreak, in early 2020. I was temporarily laid off from my job and had the time to do so. With much love, I dedicate this book to those who were adversely affected or lost their lives to this terrible virus. I am deeply grateful to all those essential workers that were on the front lines fighting for the rest of us. This includes one of my daughters who is a nurse and was right on the front lines trying to heal these patients. Your courage and strength have given the rest of us a very humbling experience of gratitude.

INTRODUCTION

* * *

I INTRODUCE MYSELF to you simply as a working man. That is because, that is what I am. I work a fulltime job in a factory. I write books, give mediumship readings, teach spiritual classes, and study and practice all spiritual needs that I have time for. I also have many other hobbies including fishing, hunting, gardening, music, and sports.

I am married to my wife of 32 years. We have two daughters, a son-in-law, a granddaughter, and a miniature Australian shepherd. My first wife and son were killed in an automobile accident. He was only three and a half years old. So, I am a family man. I take my family responsibilities very seriously, but not so seriously that I cannot sometimes step back, look, and laugh at myself.

To help you understand my writings in this book, I want to give you a little bit of my background and beliefs. When I talk about *God*, I am not talking about a person even though I may call God He, Him, etc. I believe God is *all that is*. He is the everything.

When I write about *Spirit*, this is in reference to any soul, Spirit Guide, Guardian Angel, Holy One, loved one, angel, or any other spirit coming from the other side. I will a lot of times refer to *Spirit* in a group or plural sense. I obviously do believe in God. I also believe in Jesus. I believe that Jesus truly does inspire and teach us how to find our peace (truth) on earth.

I do have a religious background in being a Christian. That is the way I was brought up. But now, with my experiences of the spiritual nature that I have had, I do not have a religion. This is by choice. I have a connection to the God Source.

I do not feel that I need a specific religion that generally has a set of rules or standards to go by. I live in a world of freedom and peace. This peace and freedom are what truly will set you free. In this place of peace, you can learn to rise above.

My life would not include anything of the spiritual nature if I did not have the afterlife experience (ALE) that I had. At least that is what I call it. I did not have a near-death experience (NDE). I had what I like to call an afterlife experience. It may have been a near-death experience. I just do not know for sure.

In this afterlife experience, I was fortunate enough to stand in God's White Light. In this White Light experience, I was told that they wanted me to know what it felt like on the other side. I owe all this experience to God and Wilma. Wilma is a family friend on the other side that guided me through this afterlife experience.

During this experience, they (all that is) gave me what I call the greatest gift of all. The gift of standing in God's White Light. I call this the gift of *knowing*. This gift changed my life, but it only let me understand what it felt like on the other side. My White Light experience did not explain how things *work* on the other side.

Since that experience, I have spent the last six years connecting to the other side. Through my connections to the God Source, Spirit Guides, Holy Ones, and loved ones, I will use what they have taught me from the other side to explain what I have learned. I believe if you want to learn about the other side, then there is no better source than the Source itself.

My main objective in this book will be to let Spirit speak for themselves. Through my process of journaling while channeling or downloading information, I have journals of information that go back for several years. These journals are notes that I got from Spirit. In them, Spirit explains not only how things work on the other side, but how using these principles of theirs can help make our life here on earth a much more fruitful experience.

So again, I say, Spirit will tell their own story. They are willing and able, so why not? This book will give you a perspective that you may have never heard before. This uniqueness is Spirit's story blended with my journaling. They have so much to say.......

FOREWORD

* * *

To my mom,
The gift of all creation is the gift of love.
It comes from the higher vibrations from above.
How much you share it and use it, is your choice.
The Source guides our soul, it has its own voice.
The light that guides you, shines on you always.
It shines on your days and nights, and even holidays.
There are times you may mourn, though
the light shines to your heart.
The soul connection remains, it is never torn apart.
As I reach down and touch you on these special days.
May you feel me and love me in your own special way.
I never really left you, as I stand by your side.
I live your days with you, still a part of your life.
I feel it only fitting to let your heart know.
I am still with you, in your heart and as my soul.

THIS VERSE WAS given to me by Reece. He is one of my Spirit
Guides. Reece had me write this down on Christmas Eve,

2019. It was a gift for his mother. Yes, Reece's mother is still here on the earth plane. I give this wonderful demonstration of love, early on, to show how Spirit is going to speak for themselves throughout this book.

PART I

• • •

Peace, Spirit Guides, The Temple and Palace

CHAPTER ONE

• • •

Intentions

IN THIS BOOK, I will put into words what my Spirit Guides, lost loved ones, souls from the other side, and the one consciousness of God have taught me in my connections. I do not really use the word meditation anymore because I just put myself into a place of openness. This openness allows me to connect to Spirit, souls, and the power of God.

There will be stories in this book that will be told as they were presented to me, by Spirit. When I say Spirit, I am referring to the one consciousness that we are all a part of. I like to call it God. This consciousness that I connect to is what is known as the other side. A lot of people call it heaven.

Souls that are on the other side live in a world that is quite like our own. They just live at a higher vibration than we do here on earth. In this world of higher vibration, these beings live in a world of love. I know this because of the afterlife experience I had in 2014. I wrote about this experience in my first book, FIFTY YEARS OF SILENCE NO MORE.

A lot of quotes, stories, and wisdom that I will write about come from a unique spirit team of mine. I call this team *blrd*. This stands for Bob (me), Lida (A Spirit Guide), Reece (A Spirit Guide), and David (My Son). When I quote Spirit throughout this book, I will give credit at the end of the quote to who gave me the information. A lot of times it will be *blrd*.

I have learned so much from these energies of light from the other side. They are always there to help us and guide us. All we need to do is allow ourselves to be a part of this God-ness. In this God-ness, anything is possible. We as human beings here on earth need to be willing to allow the unlimited possibilities that these connections allow.

I will guide you on how to make these connections. There is not an *only one way* works system when making the connection. Every person is different. So please, do what works for you. You may not even be interested in making the connections. That is okay. Reading the information alone can be rewarding and life changing.

I will be speaking from the knowledge I have gained in my real-life experiences. These experiences include my afterlife experience and connecting to Source (God). This also includes the years of learning and practicing my mediumship abilities.

I never try to pretend that I know everything. I certainly do not. I will simply tell what has been given to me. I have many more mountains to climb on this journey here on earth that we call life.

A phrase that I used a lot in my second book, BECAUSE I HAVE BEEN THERE, is "Open your mind and your heart will follow." As we open our minds, we become more at one with all that is. This gives us a better awareness. This awareness will lead us to the goal of finding our peace. In our place of peace, we can then become attuned to the unlimited possibilities that can be found in this place of God-ness.

Most people have so many questions about the other side. We seek answers to these questions through psychic mediums, books, films, meditations, etc. I have done the same thing. I have read books, watched movies and films and connected daily to the other side.

After journaling in my connections, there were a lot of times when I was just blown away! I would go back and read what my lesson was that morning and think about it for the rest of the day. Sometimes, in this time of reflection, I could download more information from my morning session and expand upon that given information. This would help me get a better understanding of some of my lessons and how they might apply to real-life situations.

This is something they have taught me, how to mark a point in time and go back to it. At that point, you can download the rest of what was given to you in that specific time and place.

The first part of this book is about how to go about finding our peace. Spirit and I will guide you and outline a way for you to go to your place of peace. This is also called *sitting in the silence*. In this place of peace, is where everything originates.

Next, we will move on to Spirit Guides. Again, Spirit and I will help you understand how to find your guides, connect to them, and learn from them. I will finish part one by taking you to the temple and the palace of light. This is a place that Spirit takes me and teaches and guides me.

Part one of this book is essentially written so that you will understand the last two parts. A lot of the next two parts of the book are written with the understanding that the reader knows about what is written in the first part.

Part two of this book is about the grief process. It is about the pain and shock associated with the loss of a loved one, traumatic event, etc. Spirit will then guide us through the process of learning to heal, live again, and how to grow spiritually. Next, they will teach us about receiving signs from the other side.

In the last part, part three, we will learn about what happens when we cross over to the other side. This will include what happens on both sides of the veil at the time of cross over. I found this information to be quite interesting.

Spirit will also explain what souls do on the other side, how things work there, and what it is like. There is a lot of mind-expanding information in this part of the book. They have taught me so much. Like I mentioned earlier, my afterlife experience only let me experience what it felt like on the other side. In this part of my journey, Spirit has taught me about how the other side works.

As you read this book, and you read a passage where Spirit is speaking, think about how this lesson might help you in your everyday life. A lot of the messages and lessons in this book explain things about the other side. They also help us in our everyday lives.

Souls from the other side (Spirit) love to help, guide, and teach us. They help spread love and awareness. They do what is best for the greater good of all. They are always there and are a part of our lives. These beings of light have given me information that literally comes straight from the Source.

Some of their messages will be in the form of wisdom. Others may be in the form of how things are on the other side. There will be lessons, and how sometimes they can be used to help us here on the earth plane. They might sometimes use a story as a teaching tool. I will let loved ones, Spirit, the

Holy Ones, and all of God-ness speak for themselves. They are teaching me so much.

My hope is that this book will help you grow spiritually and find oneness with God. Spirit will give advice on healing a grieving heart. They will teach you to find balance and peace. Very importantly, Spirit will teach you about the other side. Hopefully, this will answer so many questions for those of us seeking out answers for our own personal journey.

Spirit wants to be heard and speak for themselves. I found this uniqueness to be very educating. I certainly do not pretend that this book has all the right answers and any other perspective is wrong. I am only giving what they have given me.

I cannot guess about how things work on the other side. I can though, give what I have been given. I love the beauty in this approach. Let them speak for themselves. They have answered so many questions that I had about the other side.

I certainly understand I have a lot more to learn. I am so honored and anxious to share with you what I have already been taught. In this book, Spirit will share so many stories, lessons, love, grief, healing, and understanding about both sides of the veil.

Allow yourself to get lost in this book. Let the outside world take care of itself when you have these pages open. Allow yourself to be open to your own peace. The peace that has always been there.

The *prayer pose* is something that most of us are familiar with. I will close out this chapter with what I have learned from the Holy Ones about the prayer pose. Spirit explains the infinite bond between a mother and child.

> *In the prayer pose, the head is slightly bowed down, and the eyes are closed. This is symbolism for being at our place of peace. The hands are open with the palms and fingers*

lightly touching. This is symbolism for the two worlds coming together. Fingers are pointing upward representing higher vibration.

That is why so many people find peace in the posture of the prayer pose. The energy of both worlds gently come together and radiate peace and love in one's energy field. A mother and her child are forever bonded in this pose.

Place your hands in front of your heart and feel the connection to a child or parent on either side of the veil. It works like the infinity symbol. Here the energy of both worlds, meet and run gently through and at the heart.
★The Holy Ones

CHAPTER TWO

• • •

Finding Your Peace

EVERYONE FINDS PEACE in their own way. What works for some might not work for others. As we go through this chapter, keep this in mind. Use what works for you.

Our place of peace is the beginning of everything. Once you learn how to get there, everything else comes from that point of origination. To grow spiritually, your place of peace is like a fast track in your own development. As we move forward, we will learn some tips for finding this space of ours and let Spirit guide us in doing so.

The peace that I am talking about is the place you can learn to go to and find your space in the silence. This silence is where all things are possible. You can shed your human body and ego and start to find yourself at the soul level. At the soul level, you have access to a whole new world.

With a lot of practice, patience, and dedication, you can change your life. You can learn things from your guides, loved ones, and any other presence from the other side. In the silence, is where you can become very connected to God. Spirit mentions this in the following way.

> *A man finds his peace within, but to grow spiritually,*
> *he finds peace in 'all that is.'* ★ blrd

I cannot explain peace without mentioning prayer. Going to your place of prayer can most definitely be your place of calm. I believe prayer is a very practical and useful way of letting go. Never underestimate the power of prayer.

I also want to mention that there are other little ways to find peace. These are things to be mindful of when not in a meditative state. What I am talking about are things like having the television blaring when no one is watching it. This can fill your mind and body with noise pollution.

Wouldn't it be more relaxing to walk around in a quiet house watering indoor plants with a jug of water? Or maybe even talking to those plants. Or even better than that, saying something nice to your spouse or children. Changing small things such as these can create a much more positive and less pollutant environment.

Peace can be readily found in nature as well. Nature holds the key to teaching us about so many things. Sitting in the silence of nature can be as rewarding and soul cleansing as anything that can be found or practiced.

Poetry, literature, books, music, etc., are also ways of finding this space that we so aspire in achieving. Getting caught up in a good book can give you a release from the material world and let your imagination and soul roam freely.

As I mentioned earlier, I do not practice religion. I practice connecting with God in the silence. I go straight to the Source. I believe that churches do wonderful work, but they, for the most part, seem to have a set of rules or doctrine that they go by. Religions are also man made, not God made. Here is what Spirit gave me on one occasion regarding religion in comparison to God. I thought this to be a very profound message.

> *Religion is a taught practice.*
> *Silence is the experience.*
> *Religion is where you ask questions.*
> *Silence is where you get answers.*
> *Religion is where you are socially accepted.*
> *Silence is where you accept yourself.*
> *Religion is a badge of honor.*
> *Silence is where you honor all that is.*
> *Religion is a set of standards.*
> *Silence is limitless.*
> *Religion is a place to look for peace.*
> *Silence is peace.*
> *Now go back and replace the word, silence, with the*
> word, God. *blrd

I still remember writing this down as Spirit gave it to me. When I was told to replace *silence* with *God*, I had to stop my connection so that I could go back and see what I had written about *silence*. It was that profound. I knew they were trying to make a point about what I am writing about in this chapter.

In the silence, is where you can go for just about anything. This space that we create is so important. Most importantly, in the silence is where you can not only learn to draw near to souls on the other side, but this is where you can sit with God! Yes, that is why I believe sitting in the silence and finding your peace is such a wonderful and enlightening thing to learn and do.

I am teaching a technique of connecting for a reason. The reason is because sometimes it is easier to learn something new, with guidance. Of course, everyone will need to make their own personal adjustments.

I recently learned the following analogy while fishing in our pond that sits on our yard of several acres. As I sat there fishing, two geese flew in and landed on the water. I noticed how gracefully they were able to land and immediately be in tune with their environment on the water. They went from the environment of the air to the environment of the water with ease.

These two geese went from one world to another with elegance. They did not just drop out of the air like a bowling ball. The two of them had a rhythm. A technique that they had probably used countless times before that day.

It is the same way when we learn to connect to *all that is*. We do not just drop in like a bowling ball. We find a way that works for us. Using our own personal technique that we develop, we can go from this world to the other using a loving, smooth, graceful method. As I just mentioned a few paragraphs back, nature can teach us so much about peace.

In your meditation, or what other means you use to connect, it is important to be comfortable. Some people can go into a meditative state while jogging or doing some other type of exercise or activity. Others may be able to go into this state of mind while gardening, doing chores, mowing the lawn, etc. Do what works for you.

I always start off with a quick word of prayer and protect myself with God's White Light. A Bible verse may work, or even a poem or any other means to put you in a safe and relaxed environment. I do think it is important to take a couple deep breaths and let your shoulders relax. This lowering of the shoulders really helps in the relaxation of the body. You do not want to be tense or uncomfortable in any way.

Next, use some type of routine to slow your mind. This may be a clearing of your chakras, listening to your slowed breathing, or even picturing something like open space in your mind. Try to clear your mind and not focus on everyday problems.

Some days it will take longer than others to slow your mind. This could be due to how much sleep you got the night before, what is going on in your personal life, or a multitude of other things. You might even turn on some type of relaxing or meditative music.

If things keep running through your mind, that is okay and normal. When this happens, there are a couple of options. You can just let the thought play out and pass because that way you are not fighting the process. You are getting into a flow.

If the thought of something like, "What's for dinner?" goes through your mind; you can let it play out and make that decision so that the flow keeps going. There might be another thought following that one, but the space between them is where you start making the connection.

Once you get into the flow, the thoughts will decrease, and you will become more focused on your connection. This is when you start to get lost inside yourself. At this point, you start to lose focus on everyday items and begin to experience a release from your everyday life.

The other option to use when thoughts come through is to just mentally hit the delete button. This just simply gets rid of the thought and allows you to make the connection.

When you start getting lost in your own consciousness, you will feel very relaxed. You kind of need to get lost in your own consciousness to find your peace. You need to first get lost to be found.

You might feel out of this world or get a sense of freedom and no worries. This is an important step and may require a lot of practice. Once you start recognizing this, you have learned how to start getting to your place of peace. This is where it all starts.

As you begin to learn this part of the process, start looking for road signs along the way. This means that when you first learn how to get to your place of peace, remember how you got there. In your mind, on the way there, you might have passed a church, or seen a relative or Spirit Guide. You may have heard music, seen colors, or felt and sensed cold chills on your body.

These are the signs that you need to remember. This means the next time you connect and go to your peace you will recognize things that got you there. You will know that you are on the right track and are getting closer to your destination.

An example of this here on earth is like when a hiker goes through the woods where there are no paths. This hiker will recognize road signs along the way such as certain trees, creeks, landscapes, etc., and know that he or she is going in the right direction to a familiar place or destination. It is the same thing.

Here is something that Spirit has to say about peace.

> *Peace is like a still, calm lake. It has no ripples. All things are calm. You can sense it through your entire essence.*
> *blrd

Use your emotions when connecting to Spirit. This will make you more aware and open. In your space, you put yourself in a position of accepting, not expecting. Once there, accept what Spirit gives you. They know what you need at that specific time.

The less you put expectations on Spirit and have acceptations, the quicker you will learn and grow. They will lead you to where you need to be. You need to be willing to surrender, release, and let Spirit guide you.

Also, the more you think thoughts about love and happiness the better your connection will be. On the other side, it is all about love. When you are thinking thoughts of love, you are aligning your vibration to the vibration of the other side. This higher vibration of love is what encompasses *all that is,* the God-ness. Here are a few things that Spirit has to say about this part of the process.

> *Do not think, just be, when with Spirit. Do not expect, accept. Expectations can lead to disappointment with Spirit. Acceptations will lead to what is meant to be. There are no ground rules with Spirit, only the rule of not expecting.*
>
> *To find your answers, you need to reach far and deep, but not outward, inward. Your answers are not in someone else, they are in you. Once you find yourself, then you can project that peace outward onto others.*
>
> *A man must find peace inside himself, not inside someone else. Allow and accept others. This gives you freedom that will balance your own space.* *blrd

In these previous statements from Spirit, I want to point out that part of your peace is also found by not just being in your place of silence. It also includes accepting people here on earth just as they are. Do not try to make people what you want them to be, let them be them. Do not expect other people to be something that they are not. Let them be who they are and accept them for that and do not try to change them.

This goes for how we want to live our life too. To find our peace we need to be who we want to be, not what others want us to be. We do this using our own free will. If we are not hurting anyone, then there is no reason for us not to use our free will in finding our own truth.

I believe that Jesus taught us about peace, freedom, and truth. He talked a lot about these topics in the New Testament of the Bible. I believe that Jesus did speak of so many things to teach us how to find our peace here on earth. Here is an example of what I am talking about.

> *Finding your peace will answer a lot of questions and solve many problems in your life. Because, ultimately, peace is the answer to everything. This new place will lead to being at one with all that is (God). Jesus taught us this.*
>
> *A lot of people go to church seeking their peace. Connecting to the God Source in the silence is peace.*
> *blrd

Finding peace has a couple of key ingredients. They are love and forgiveness. These two ingredients of love and forgiveness give us a sense of balance. This balance is important in the process. Love is the answer, but forgiveness is the motivator. If you have balance from these two ingredients, then you have peace.

Spirit gave me a formula representing this fundamental part of finding peace. In it, they used a math sketch to make it easy to understand. Obviously, they did so because they understand that I like math. This is a good example of Spirit knowing what to use, and how to use it, because they understand how our own individual minds work.

To teach me this lesson, Spirit used the PI symbol. The number for PI is 3.14. It is an infinite number, meaning it goes on for eternity. Just for fun, I will also throw a little numerology into the mix. In numerology, the number 3.14 translates to an 8. Of course, the number eight is also a symbol for infinity.

If your love and forgiveness are flowing, this gives you peace. This peace is what leads you to your own personal truth (peace) that Jesus so often spoke about. This peace/truth is an eternal blessing. It is infinite. I really like this example.

Pi Symbol

Following up on this sketch, Spirit gave me the following messages.

> *Your peace is your sanctuary of truth.* ★blrd
>> *As you crest the top of a mountain, you feel a sense of accomplishment. It gives you a feeling of self-worth. You are proud of yourself. You feel a sense of inner peace.*
>> *It is the same way when connecting. You learn to find your peace. In this space, you realize that you are not perfect. You accept this. Once you learn how to get there, you can go there anytime, or when needed.* ★blrd

In the previous quote, you realize that you are not perfect. This is such an important point in finding peace. You are at peace when you understand that you are not perfect and the other people around you are not either. You do not try to be perfect. In a place of peace, you simply ARE!

To grow spiritually, and to get better at being in your place of peace takes practice. Practice will help you get there in your meditative state. Then you can learn to take your peace with you everywhere you go. Spirit teaches us this in the following story.

> *As the old man lay there, at the end of his life cycle, he was being comforted by his daughter. In doing so, she asked him, "Daddy, what was your secret? You always found peace in all the places you went in your life, and in all the things you did. How did you achieve this?" As the old man took his last breath, he said, "Honey, the best things in life are simple. I never found peace in any of those places. I always took it with me." *blrd*

Once you get in a routine of going to this space you created, you will start to understand that it is a place of timelessness. That is how things work on the other side. It is a sense of timelessness that can only be found in peace and balance. Here is what Spirit has to say about the topic of timelessness.

> *Peace is not measured by standards or a stick. Peace on this side of the veil is the equivalent of the timelessness on the other side. This timelessness, on either side, is your freedom. Your peace is found by finding that place of timelessness on this side of the veil.*
>
> *Freedom is the peace found in finding your own truth that lies within. Once you learn to find this freedom of truth that comes from within, you have been born again. You have found a new beginning that was there all along.* *blrd*

Never worry about what other people might think or say when you are on your journey of finding your peace. This is your peace, not theirs! This work is not *out there*. It is freedom!

In your sacred space, you understand just how important you are. You are yourself; not what others might want you to be. Here, you can learn from your higher self. This is a process in which you are learning at the soul level. Here is what Spirit had to say about being you.

The higher self guides us and keeps us in balance. In your place of peace, go to your higher self. Here, you will understand that you are love and balance. Surrender to your higher self.

This balance of truth and love is your peace. Everything you need is there. By surrendering, you will find balance in all that is and all that is to be. Here, it is all about you. And then,

You know that you matter.
You forgive yourself.
You love.
You accept.
You learn.
You focus.
You find balance.
You accept yourself.
You never doubt how important you are.
You ARE... ★blrd

Hopefully, the information in this chapter will help you along in your own personal journey. Later in the book, this information about peace will help you understand the content of those upcoming chapters. My guides and others will speak about it.

Sitting in the silence can open you up to an awareness that was always there, but maybe had not been opened and used. Finding your peace in the silence can help you grow spiritually. It can also help you understand that other people have their own free will to be what they want to be, and our job is to simply accept them.

As I close out this chapter, I will leave you with the wisdom of Spirit. Here, they so fittingly and simply describe a man at peace.

Someone who has found their peace, understands that others may find theirs differently. ★blrd

CHAPTER THREE

* * *

Spirit Guides

EVERYONE HAS SPIRIT Guides. These are beings on the other side that are there to help us and guide us in our everyday lives. There are different types of guides. Some are temporary helpers, sent to get us through hurdles or struggles in our lives. Others can be lifelong guides that are with us from the womb of our mother to the day that we cross over.

When I say cross over, I am talking about the day that our physical body dies, and we cross over to the other side (heaven). This is when our soul leaves the body and continues with its journey. Some of these lifelong guides will also be with us on the other side.

Our Spirit Guides help us in our journey here on the earth plane. Here, they try to steer us in the right direction. At times in our lives, there will be a fork in the road. One of our guides might step forward at this point and try to steer us in the direction that would be most beneficial to our spiritual growth.

If you are not yet aware of or in contact with your guides, you might just get a sense of knowing or intuition. This, more than likely, is them at work. They are trying to connect with you at the soul level.

On the other side, our guides work with us and tell us how and what we need to do to grow spiritually and raise our vibration. Our ego is absent. This means that everything is done with, and through, love.

We do not get offended or upset when we are being guided. This is because there is an understanding. This understanding is a combination of balance, peace, love, and knowing.

Everything works together harmoniously. The light of God, colors, sounds, guides, souls, and all that is, have a common purpose that works through the harmonious melody of love. Spirit describes the harmony of love on the other side.

> *On the other side, the colors are alive. They are alive with harmonic notes, vibrations, and love. There is only harmony in this love. Let the colors of your chakras, spinning in your body, play a tune of love throughout your body. Allow them to do their job. Let the vibrational energies of your chakras work in unison to play a tune of higher vibration.*
>
> *In doing so, these higher frequencies and vibrations send healing energy throughout your body. This is the buzz of the higher vibrational learning that is made available to all who are willing to accept. Let your vibrations of love sing out.* ★blrd

Learning how to connect with these Spirit Guides generally takes practice. I do believe that everyone possesses the ability to make these connections. To meet your Spirit Guides, you first need to learn how to go to your place of peace that I wrote about in the last chapter. Once you have learned to go to your peace, then you have opened the door to the unlimited possibilities of the other side.

In your place of peace, ask your guides to step forward. This is usually in a meditative state of mind. In the beginning, it will most likely be easier to ask one guide to step forward. You can do this out loud or in your mind only.

Some people will see their guide, others may hear them, sense them, or feel them. There is no *one way* that works for everyone. Use whatever works for you.

The next step is important anytime you are connecting with Spirit. Accept whatever comes to you. Do not try to change it. Spirit is giving you things for a reason. Spirit will lead you to where you need to be.

So, in other words, do not expect anything from Spirit. Always be in a receptive mode of acceptance. I cannot stress this point enough. Acceptance instead of expectance will speed up your development in meeting your guides.

Once you have requested a guide to step forward, accept whatever is given to you. This can include appearance, how they talk or communicate, how they are dressed, etc. Also accept whatever name they give you when you ask for it. If they say their name is Elvis, then go with Elvis. If they do not give you a name, that is okay. They may give it to you later, or maybe never at all.

In this first instance of connection with your guide, tell them you are interested in what is good for the greater good of all. Tell your guide that you are asking him/her to help you in your connections, teach you, and guide you. That is what they are there for. It is their job to help you.

They love you and want what is best for you. Always be very loving, polite, and show gratitude. Thank them for anything they give you. The more you show gratitude and love towards them, the better your connection will be. When you connect over and over with your guides, just talk to them as if they are there. The reason for this is because they are there!

It can take many sessions to meet your guides. It may not happen the first time or two that you try. That is okay. You will make the connection with them when you are ready. They know when this is, so please do not get frustrated if you are having a hard time making the connection.

There may be times when you are connecting, and you see someone who is not familiar to you. Keep in mind this may be one of your guides. First, see if you feel comfortable with this energy. If so, ask them to step forward. Ask them if they are your guide. This could very well be the beginning of a very intimate and loving relationship with a spirit that has stepped forward for you because they knew you were ready.

You may find that you have different guides for different areas of your life. Some of them may come and go, but there usually will be one or more who stay with you all the time. Personally, I have several guides. I also call each one by name.

I have a guide that I call Mademoiselle. She is what I call my mother guide. She has been with me since the beginning when I was in the womb. Mademoiselle is a light brown skinned, African woman.

She guides me like a motherly figure who always has and always will watch out for me. She has shown me many instances in my life when she was there for me. Of course, at that time, I did not even realize it was happening and that she was there.

One case was when I was about five years old and was playing with a box of odds and ends that I found in one of the closets of our home. In this box, was an electric plug that you would plug into a wall. It was cut and frayed on the end. It was about two feet long. Unknowingly, as a child, I plugged it into the wall and the frayed end of the wire started dancing around from the electric current.

She told me that she was there when it happened and protected me. As she told me this, I remembered that my intuition told me to grab it by the plug and not by the wire as it was happening. I did so, and that was that. Although, I can still remember the smell that the dancing electric wire made.

Another instance she told me about was a time when I let one of our teenage daughters move one of our cars. This was in a grassy area in our yard. She was about fifteen years old at the time and did not have her driver's license yet. Trying to be a good father, and boost her confidence, I decided to let her move a few vehicles around in the yard before we had guests arriving for a party.

I directed and guided her as she was parking one of the vehicles. I was standing next to one vehicle, as I guided her to park next to it. She had the car in reverse and was backing it in next to the car I was standing beside. After she got close to the spot to park, I had her stop and started talking to her.

As we finished talking, I told her to pull forward and put it in park. As she accelerated, the car was still in reverse and she started to smash me between the two vehicles. Luckily, she hit the brake pedal just in time and serious injury or possible death was avoided. I will never forget how close of a call that it was. Mademoiselle let me know that she had been with me in this instance.

Mademoiselle has been there for me like a Guardian Angel at times and gave me comfort and guidance when I needed it. Even though at the time, I did not know it. She is a guide that is with me in my everyday life. Whether I just need a nudge a certain way, need comfort, or just living my everyday life, she is there.

Another guide that I have is Red Eagle. He is my spiritual counselor. Red Eagle is a Native American. He has dark black hair that is about shoulder length. He wears war paint on his face and wears a chest armor made of bones. He also wears a full headdress of feathers.

Sometimes he is on a horse, and other times he is not. Red Eagle always has a serious look on his face. He likes to get straight down to business.

Whenever I need spiritual guidance, he makes himself known in my connections. I do not see him every day, or even that often. I know when I see him that he has something important to show or teach me.

Gandolf is the name of one of my other guides. He dresses and looks like a wise man in a white robed attire. He has long stringy white/grey hair and has a medium build. Gandolf shows up more often than Red Eagle. He is one of my teachers.

Whenever I have a question or I have asked for something in connecting, Gandolf eventually comes to give me guidance. He might even show up to teach me something else that I need to learn. When he appears, he just stands and looks at me. He waits for me to ask him why he is there.

Sometimes it can take more than one connection to figure out what his lesson is. Gandolf is a guide who also has a unique purpose in my spiritual development, which is the life I am living here on earth. Here is some wisdom that Gandolf gave me in 2019, as he was helping me in my spiritual growth.

> *Be humble, kind, and patient. Listening and acting can be better than words. Always send out peace. Peace and a lesson can be found in everything you receive from me.*

Touch lightly but leave a big imprint. What you say
does not need to be spoken loudly. Let it resonate out. Let
it be a soothing message of peace and love.

So here we have a Spirit Guide of mine, Gandolf, suggesting how I use the information here on earth that he gave me from the other side. How cool is that?

Jerry is a guide of mine who patches me up when I need it. By this, I mean that when life hits me hard, or I am going through a rough patch, Jerry is there to encourage me to get back at it. He is like a cornerman for a boxer. He patches me up between rounds.

Jerry simply looks and dresses like an average person. He has a semi-bushy grey beard that is not too long, wears a ballcap, and has glasses. When he shows up, he does not say anything. This is an instance where there is no communication between me and my guide, but I sense what he is there for.

I do not see Jerry that often, but I understand why he is there when he shows up. He does not give me information or guidance like my other guides. He simply patches me up and sends me back in. When I do see him, I know that something in my life might need some guidance from another guide or source. Jerry is just like a flag or sign letting me know that I am not alone on my journey.

A recent addition to my council of guides is Lida. I only started noticing him in the last year or two. Lida moves in a very methodical and balanced way.

He is an old soul. He is one of the elders on the other side. I call these elders, *gatekeepers*. He is very respected and revered on the other side and is somewhat like a Holy One. Lida is very highly evolved.

He wears a black cape that has a large collar. It reminds of something you would see a college chancellor wear at a graduation ceremony. His head is odd shaped. At times, I am not even sure if he is human. Although, when I do see him presenting himself to me as a human, he is tall, thin, and has very magical eyes.

He is like a counselor who sits me down and gives me lessons. Lida teaches me about the other side and what I need to work on in my connections. Right now, Lida is my main source to the other side. He not only teaches me about the other side, but he is helping me with my spiritual growth as well. Lida tells me that I must become whole, spiritually, to further my development with the other side.

His energy is strong because of his high vibration. It took me awhile to get used to it. He is with me a lot. I see him almost daily. Lida is who I work with on my spiritual development more than anyone else.

He can also be a goofball at times. He is not all work and no play. He loves to work me, but he also lets me know that there is a time for play. Spirit does like to have fun, just like we do.

The following is something Lida told me Christmas week, 2018. He talks about the upcoming year and he could not have been any more accurate. It was my most spiritually growing year since I was fortunate enough to stand in the White Light of God in 2014.

> *It is going to be an amazing year. This has always been in the making, but you are just now ready. Your energy and alignment have progressed. Seek and you shall find. Ask and it will be given. Look no further than yourself for your treasure. I am with you and available 24/7. This is an important part of your journey.*

In the previous paragraph, Lida basically explains to me that in the year 2019 all I need to do is ask and I will get my answers.

I listened to his advice and asked a lot about how things are like on the other side. This is an important point. The last chapters of this book reflect answers that I asked questions about.

The following twelve months after these messages from Lida, my spiritual growth passed even my expectations. I am honored and blessed to have such a high being of light, like Lida, personally helping me along in my journey!

My other guide is a young man named Reece. He helps me understand what Lida is trying to teach me if I do not understand. Reece is regular build to thin with darker hair. He is not overly tall, but not short in stature. Reece presents himself to me as 18-20 years old.

So yes, since Reece helps me around Lida a lot, I do see him quite often. One of the biggest things Reece does for me is telling me when I need to go to my peace. If I am out of sorts, he makes me focus and go to my place of peace.

It is intriguing how I happened upon Reece. I am in a gratitude group with other parents who have lost children. His mother is in this group. When I was giving his mother a reading, he told me that we were from the same soul group and that he is one of my guides.

It really blew me away! I never expected that. I believe this story is a good example of do not expect, accept. Reece really plays an important role in my spiritual development, alongside Lida.

After you have figured out who your guide or guides are, start building a relationship with them. In doing so, tell them what you would like them to help you with. You can ask them for guidance on issues in your life. Ask them questions. They will hear you.

You might not get your answer right away, but you generally will get an answer. You can ask them a question and then ask for a sign as an answer in the next day. An example would be, "Mademoiselle, am I heading in the right direction on my spiritual journey? If so, could you please give me a sign, as a feather, in the next day?"

One of the coolest things about working with your guides is that they already know what is in your mind and how your mind works. They will use this information to help you understand what they are communicating to you. An example of this would be; If they show you an apple, and every time you see an apple it makes you think about a doctor, then your guide may be telling you to go see your doctor and get a check-up.

Again, some people will see an apple, some will hear the word apple, etc. Everyone is different. The point being is they will use information that you understand. When something like this happens, it is the beginning of the dialogue that you will need to set up with your guide to help strengthen the connection.

You can also use your guides to help you connect to other souls as well. You may have lost an old friend and are wanting to contact them on the other side. The first thing you need to do is set the intention. This means to let your guide know who you are wanting to communicate with on the other side. Simply ask your guide to connect you to who you are wanting to hear from.

You may do this in advance of your connection, even a day or so before you connect. This can be done in your mind or aloud. It does not matter. Your guide will hear you.

Once your guide has a system in place with you, he will then be able to let those you want to connect with know how your system of communication works. This will make your connection with them better.

Think of calling upon your guide as using an old rotary dial phone. Simply dial zero and call the operator. Your guide, obviously, is the operator. It works something like this; Guide: "Please hold while I make the connection." It really is that simple.

Lastly, never forget to thank your guide and/or whoever it is that you connected to. This is important. It takes their energy as well as yours to make the connection. You are meeting them in the middle. They lower their vibration as you raise your vibration. This is what enables the connection. You can raise your vibration by going to your place of peace.

We have learned to go to and find our place of peace and connect to loved ones and Spirit. We now have a general idea of what Spirit is, and how to get there. So, let us now start to put these practices to use and let Spirit guide us. Let us continue our journey and go to the temple and palace.

CHAPTER FOUR

• • •

The Temple and Palace

THE TEMPLE AND palace are places that I go when I connect to Spirit. I meet with my Spirit Guides in these places, along with loved ones, Holy Ones, and all others. These two places are a good example of what I wrote about earlier in finding your place of peace. They are like a road sign or marker for me.

I know when I arrive at one of them, something magical can always happen. Going to either one of these places helps a lot. Especially if I am having a day where my connection is slow or not as good as I want or need it to be. When I refer to the temple and palace, later in the book, this chapter will help you understand what I am writing about.

As I go through and explain about these two places, let your imagination run wild. Let go and let Spirit captivate you and show how if you are willing, then anything is possible. This chapter is a good example of how you can put your ego (mind) to rest and journey at the soul level. At the soul level, all things are possible.

I do not go to these two places one hundred percent of the time. I usually go there for my guides to teach me a lesson or give advice. The type of things that I would typically get from *blrd*. I have learned so much about the other side in the temple, and especially the palace. They truly are my places of learning.

I will give some of what I have learned there in this chapter, but later in the book I will go into detail about what Spirit has taught me about the other side. I have learned about the other side from Spirit at these two places.

I do not go to either one of these places when I am giving a reading to a client (sitter). When I give readings, I just go straight to the soul that is wanting to talk with my sitter. This process happens after I set the intention of making the connection for my sitter with my Spirit Guides. They usually find these souls for me for my readings. Also, just by setting the intention to connect to souls for a specific sitter, these energies from the other side can pick up on that signal and just show up on their own.

There are also times when I connect with my guides and we are not in the temple or palace. This usually happens when I first start my session. I will ask who is here for the day and sometimes one of my guides will just appear. Depending on who it is, I can tell what they are there for. If it is Red Eagle, then I know that he is there to give me a lesson in the spiritual nature.

I know right away when I see one of my guides appear very quickly that they are there for a reason. This means they are there waiting on me and have something that I need to work on in my spiritual development.

I love when this happens because it catches me off guard. It really helps with the flow because it was not something that

I was expecting. This way it just gives me a sense of validation that it was not something that my mind came up with. It is real.

First, let me explain about the temple. As I get to my place of peace in my connection and I arrive there, I feel as if I am home. It is a place that I have been to so many times. I feel comfortable when arriving there. This sense of being at home helps me in my flow and strengthens the connection.

The temple sits on a lot just like any other building would on a street in Anytown, USA. There is a large tree that sits on the lot. It sits on the right side as you are facing the building. The temple looks a lot like a church, both from the inside and out.

There are a set of concrete steps that lead up to the front door which is elevated to the level of about eleven steps. The front stoop is not that large. It is around seven feet by seven feet. The front door has a handle made of metal and is arched at the top. It has a pull chain right above the handle that you pull to unlatch and open the door. Also, the front door is very weathered and cracked. It is made of wood and looks like it needs a paint job.

As I enter the building, right in front of me, in an open area, are two souls. They are always there waiting on me and to greet me. One of them looks like a monk and the other looks like Gandhi, so that is what I call him.

When I get to them in the middle of the open area up front in the temple and arrive where these two souls are standing, there is a, white, wash basin. It is standing freely on the floor in front of the monk and Gandhi. It looks like a white, free standing, pedestal sink.

I then splash water from this basin on my face and dip my hands into the water and rinse them off. Gandhi then hands me a white cotton hand towel that I use to dab my face and hands to gently dry them off. After I have finished with the towel, I briefly communicate with the monk and Gandhi. It is done telepathically. I thank them and send them love, as they also do me.

As we stand in this front area of the temple and look around, there are stadium seats that elevate and cover the building like a horseshoe type stadium appearance. These seats are on the right side as you enter. Thus, the front part looks like a stage area.

There are no lights in the temple. It seems to have only natural lighting. There are a couple of stained-glass windows that are in front of the staging area. They are on the left as you go in.

Sometimes there is a guide that appears for me at the white basin of water. When this happens, I know there is something pending, and they have a lesson. It can be Lida or any of my other guides.

A lot of times it is Reece. He is usually there waiting on me when there is something in store for me that day in the palace. Reece acts as my guide interpreter; his guidance truly helps me a lot.

Sometimes in the temple, there will be a guide, elder, angel, or other being that will speak. When this happens, there are souls sitting in the arena/stadium type seating. Reece and I will then take our seat and listen with the other souls. A lot of times my son, David, is with Reece. It is a very enlightening experience. There are good life lessons and soul growth lessons taught by whoever is speaking.

Other times, after drying my face and hands off in front of the monk and Gandhi, I will continue past them and go to the back door. There are three marble steps that lead to the back door. They go the length of the building. It seems a lot like what you would see at the front of a church.

This is the door that leads to the palace. The door looks a lot like the front door of the temple. It is made of wood and has a metal handle. It is also arched at the top. This door looks nice and freshly painted. Above the handle, is a metal thumb lever that has a gold or brass appearance. It opens very easily.

As I enter the palace, there is an area that is like an atrium or entry area. For some reason there are stainless steel racks sitting there with green plants. I believe these are herbs that represent things of a healing nature.

In this entryway area is where loved ones can be waiting for me. I get the chance to reminisce with them and share love. They are always happy to see me as I am them. Sometimes my dad is there, other times my son, other times my first wife or other loved ones.

After sharing in this reminiscing, a guide may then appear. This is when we will leave the entry area and head down a corridor. This corridor is like a hallway or tunnel. This hallway leads to the palace of light.

The palace is where the Holy Ones reside and teach. It seems that only the beings of the highest light are there. Here is where the higher vibrational learning, love, and true peace reside. The palace is my place of learning about the other side.

I mentioned earlier that I work in a factory. I work on an assembly line, which is repetitive motion and work. With years of practice, I have developed a system of what I call *going into trance*. In this trance state, I can be in both worlds at the same time. I am focused on where I am at on the other side, but somehow aware of what I am doing on my job in the factory.

I feel as if I am in slow motion and the rest of the world is at a higher speed. This is me slowing my mind down, thus raising my vibration. This is how I go to the other side anytime that I want while working.

If someone talks to me while in this trance state, it is like I can hit the pause button for the other side, answer that person, and continue back into trance. I also wear a wireless headset that I play theta wave meditation music on to put me in the right mindset. It also drowns out background noise from the factory floor.

One time in this trance state at work, I met a Guardian Angel of mine. This had never happened before or since this wonderful connection. As I was walking down the hallway in the palace with Reece, to meet up with Lida, it started to happen.

First, a being of high vibration and light started walking towards us. I do not think that this angel had a gender, but she presented herself as female. She had dark hair, that was nicely done and had a blue diamond shaped sapphire on her chest. This sapphire seemed to be about the size of a softball. She let me know telepathically that she was my Guardian Angel and that her name was Athena.

As she approached Reece and me, she seemed to glow. She radiated a light of wellness off her translucent form of a body. There were different colors associated with her and her presence.

I did not get much information from her, just a sense of awe and knowing. She seemed to just want to introduce herself to me and send me love. Athena is a being of high understanding and light. I believe she wanted me to know that not only are Spirit Guides, elders, and Holy Ones in the palace, but Guardian Angels as well.

As Athena passed by me on my left side in the hallway, other beings started to approach. At first, I was a little confused, but with their telepathic help I started to really flow and understand. Then a being who shined red light from its translucent body approached me, also passing by me on my left side.

As this being was in the process of approaching and passing me, it conveyed to me telepathically what my strong suits were in the base or root chakra. This chakra is represented by the color red. The base chakra is located at the base of the spine. The chakras are the seven energy points in our bodies.

Next, a being came representing what I was strong in at the second chakra level, the navel chakra. It is represented by the color of orange. Then it was the third (yellow) solar plexus chakra, followed by the fourth (green) heart chakra, fifth (light blue) throat chakra, sixth (indigo) third eye chakra, and the seventh (purple) crown chakra.

As each being of light passed by, it shined its appropriate color and chakra. This being would also let me know what my strong suits were in that specific area of my life. At the end of this cycle, Reece and I continued walking down the hallway.

We had just figured out that I was in the process of being given a life review. It was like a test run so I could understand how things work in the palace when souls are crossing over. I will never forget Reece saying, "I can't believe they are letting you do this." He was so excited for me, as was I.

It seemed that Lida was at the end of the hallway waiting for us, but something on the left side of the hallway caught my attention. It was an open doorway. Light was flickering out from the room, through the door, into the hallway. It was the kind of light that an old reel to reel projector would put out. That is how I recognized it. I was then called by my intuition to enter this room, so I did.

After entering the room, I was seated in a chair facing the front. Lida and Reece were there but in the back of the room. They were there as viewing guests only. There were other beings of light (angels) there to assist me. This was a room for doing life reviews.

I was taken there to experience how and where a life review happens. It was all part of the process, just like the Guardian Angel, Athena, and the other beings of light explaining my strong points in the chakras. I was being shown and experiencing the process of how certain things happen after cross over.

Reece was right earlier. How lucky was I to be able to go through this procedure? And to top it all off, this was all happening while I was in trance working an assembly line in a factory!

Up to this point, I had not encountered anything negative, only positive feedback. I am far from perfect, so I thought "Here it comes." It never did though.

Of course, this was just a demonstration of how the process works. Instead of getting negative feedback during this mock review, I was instead shown compassion, love, and given an understanding. I finished this review process up with a sense of belonging and understanding, along with love.

With years of practice of going into trance, while doing repetitive motion work on an assembly line in a factory, I have gotten quite good at it. It is like I have the ability and opportunity to leave work at any time I feel like it. It is a fun and exciting thing to do. I believe everyone has the capability to do this as well, with the right work ethic, practice, and attitude.

Always remember, there are no limits when it comes to the spirit world. The only limits are the ones that we allow our minds (ego) to give ourselves. These limits are self-imposed. Soul growth comes from our place of peace. There, the opportunities and possibilities are limitless. Spirit talks about peace in the following message.

In the silence, lose track of time and you will find yourself.
Here, walk where no other man walks and open yourself
to all that is, peace. ★blrd

I have so many more stories involving the temple and palace, but I will tell them later in the book. This is when I will relay to you, the reader, what Spirit has told me about the other side. Not just what souls do there, but how the process works and what it is like!

PART II

• • •

Grief, Loss, Healing, and Signs

CHAPTER FIVE

● ● ●

Grief and Loss

WHAT IS GRIEF and loss? That is a good question and calls for perspective. There are different kinds of grief and there are different types of loss.

Grief can be associated with the period following the death of a loved one. It can also be something within one's heart that is associated with loss, but of a different nature. This could be the loss of someone's personal life due to a life changing event, such as being the caretaker for another person.

In this chapter, I will discuss different forms of grief and loss. As always, everyone's personal journey is different. I will go into the different perspectives of grief and loss, but at a broad range view.

When it comes to loss, I can speak from experience. As a young man, I lost my first wife and three-year-old son to a drunk driver. Also, in this time period of my life, my father went into a coma for three months. After coming out of his coma, he was an invalid and had the mind of a small child for the rest of his life, which lasted about fifteen more years. So yes, I do understand loss and the grief that is associated with it, first-hand.

I was working, as a manager, in a grocery store one evening when I got that dreaded phone call from the hospital. When I arrived at the hospital, a police officer informed me that my twenty-two-year old wife had been killed in an automobile accident. I remember turning around and hitting the wall with my fist. My legs felt like rubber and I immediately went into shock.

I asked the officer where my son was. I was told he had been airlifted to another hospital. Twenty-four hours later, my son, David, died in my arms as he took his last breath.

My father had to be taken care of, as an invalid, that could not speak, walk, or even communicate, for the next fifteen years by my mother, siblings, spouses, and me. This was a long-term event that did not just happen and have closure right away. My wife and son, I lost quickly. My father, I lost over a period of a decade and a half. This right here is an example of two different kinds of loss of a loved one.

I want to state, in my opinion, that losing a child is one of the worst forms of loss that there is. For those people out there that have lost children, I get it. I understand your loss and grief. This kind of grief is hard to overcome, but it can be done.

So, I do understand trauma, loss, and grief very well and first-hand. I do not have to ask Spirit about these things. I truly have the experiences of learning these things the hard way. Spirit does though understand events like these and gives an eternal perspective. I am simply telling my story.

I believe that a lot of people who are on the outside looking in, when it comes to life events like these, simply do not have the perspective as someone who has walked in those shoes.

People care and try to comfort others who have had loss. But if they have not been there, then they do not fully understand the loss and grief associated with certain events. People do try to help all they can, in this frantic paced world and environment that we live in, but it is not the same. Not unless you have walked down those paths.

If you are out in public and see someone who is taking care of a severely handicapped person or someone who has very acute mental disabilities, you probably do not understand the situation. Unless you have been there, then it is unlikely you can understand the depth of the situation. The caretakers of the kind of people I mentioned are put under a lot of stress, worry, anxiety, etc. Not to mention, that their lives have also been altered in a large way.

Someone from the outside looking in could possibly think, "Oh, that person is severely handicapped, but they are nicely dressed and look nice." They might even be nice and say something positive to that person. That is where it ends for them. They are free to go on with their life and do normal things. It is wonderful that they make the effort to be courteous and caring, but it is not the same as being tied to this kind of situation.

The caretaker though, is the one that put those nice clothes on the disabled person and got them cleaned up and presentable. It does not end there for them. This is just a public appearance. They then continue with their every day, abnormal, life. They go home and do the behind the scenes things that no one knows about unless they have walked in those shoes.

This is not a crack on those who do not know. It is simply an example of how when bad things happen to someone, they can happen in so many ways. Everyone's path is different. You need to live it to understand it.

The people living with these acute mental disabilities and/
or severe handicaps, I tip my hat to you. Your journey is far
different than the journey of most people. Your journey does
matter. You matter. You are important. You are love.

Loss can come in many different forms. Loss does not mean
that you have necessarily lost a loved one. It can mean that you
lost having a normal life. Situations like these can certainly be
just as stressful and hard on someone as losing a loved one can
be. Losing your ability to function normally due to a severe
handicap is a form of loss. Just as a person who has been abused,
neglected, etc., everyone does not have the same experience
when it comes to loss and grief. It has a very wide audience.

I can remember after losing my wife and son, it felt like
my chest was empty. It felt like my heart was gone and had
been ripped out of my body. When I was in my truck driving
somewhere, I could not even have the radio on. My mind
literally could not take anymore. There was no room for
anything else. I was barely breathing, let alone living a normal
life.

All I wanted was for time to pass. I kept thinking thoughts
like, "In five years, ten years, or twenty years, maybe things
will be better." I just wanted to escape the life that I was
presently living in. I wanted to live in a world that was not so
painful.

This place of loss I learned at the early age of twenty-two
was a place that I did not want to be. I just wanted it to go away,
like a bad dream. Well, obviously, it does not work that way.

I remember a story a few weeks after losing my wife and
son. I was working at the grocery store one evening and I was
talking to one of the other managers of the store. We were
standing behind a set of metal swinging doors that had small
windows. These doors lead from the sales floor of the store to

the back part of the store where inventory of merchandise was kept.

I looked out into the sales area of the store and saw a young woman that looked like my first wife. I stopped mid conversation and quickly walked out to the sales area. I was almost running. I was thinking, "It didn't really happen, she is still alive. Where is my son, David?"

I was getting ready to hug her and ask her where David was and right before doing so, that is when it hit me. I quickly realized that it was not her. It was someone who looked like her, from behind.

This is an example of how in a time of loss and/or serious grief, we are not our normal selves. We are in a state of shock and our minds are so cluttered with pollution and grief that we sometimes cannot function normally. I believe this is normal. I used this personal example to help you understand that it is okay and acceptable to go through this kind of experience. No one is perfect.

There are going to be bumps in the road for us in this personal journey of ours here on earth. There will be peaks and valleys. It seems that the valleys go a lot deeper for some than they do for others. People who have had bad things happen to them have a different kind of journey than those who have not.

This is where it is important for us not to be envious of them, but to be thankful that they did not have to experience the bottom part of the valleys, as we did. Somewhere in these valleys there is a lesson for us to learn. It might be a hard way to learn, but it is part of our journey. Spirit talks about this in a couple of different ways.

> *Sometimes the bumps in the road of your journey are just a leap to the next peak. They are there to get your attention. There are always more peaks ahead. The peaks are there*

to help you climb out of the valley. There is growth and a lesson in every story. ★David

Yesterday is not about what was wrong. It is about what you have learned. No one or circumstance is perfect. Even the soul is not perfect. It is here to learn, sometimes through these hard life lessons. ★blrd

I believe that the people we lose are sent to us as a gift. They are a gift of love and beauty. They were put into our lives for a reason, by the Source. This Source is the creation of all love. We are eternally connected to these people with a bond that is never broken.

I love the following example I received. The topic of signs and crossing over will be discussed more in the coming chapters, but I do believe that this is the right place, here, to let Spirit explain this important subject. If you are grieving the loss of a loved one, especially a child, then let your emotions flow as you read this story.

There is this little five-year-old boy who crosses over into God's White Light. An angel asks him why he is carrying a bag and tells the boy that material things are not needed where he is now.

The little boy tells the angel that the bag is full of lessons learned. The angel tells him that he only lived five years, and asks him how many lessons could he have learned? In response, the boy says, "I taught the nurse that she can't save everyone. I taught my siblings to cherish the moments. I taught my mom and dad how much they can love someone."

Next, the angel asks him why he needs the bag if it only has non-material things in it. The boy then tells the angel that it is full of butterflies and anytime that he goes to visit any of these people he is going to let a butterfly

loose so they can remember what he taught them. The angel says, "Welcome home son, I have someone that I want you to meet." ★blrd

One of the biggest things I learned from this painful part of my life is that the damage is done. There is no taking it back. People who have had bad things happen to them carry that with them for the rest of their lives.

I am talking about loss of loved ones, abuse victims, neglect, and any other type of negative impact on one's life. Once this damage is done, it is done. You find a way to go on living, but it is a different kind of life. Over time these wounds will start to heal, but the scar will always be there.

But, as we head into the rest of this part of the book, I will show how there is hope. There is always hope. I will not only continue to share my story, but I will let Spirit help explain things and give their take on loss, grief, and healing.

I can most certainly give people hope. I can do this because of my afterlife experience. Remember, I know what it feels like on the other side! I know what kind of love people are experiencing after they cross over. Keep this in mind as you learn about grief and healing in this part of the book. I hope that this part of the book will help set your heart free and bring you peace.

Again, once bad things have happened to us, there is no changing it. At that point, we own it. Spirit gives a little bit of advice on this.

Learning to accept things is not always easy but trying to change the story will not make the story go away. ★blrd

This previous short lesson reminds us that the damage is done. The story from the past will not change, but we do have the ability to change the story of our future. We can do this with our free will. If you are suffering from loss, this probably does not seem to help right now, but it will as we go through the rest of the book.

Everyone is different. Just like in finding our peace, everyone does not find it the same way. We need to go through our process of grief and loss in our own way. Grieving is normal. There is nothing wrong with grieving and crying. It is a natural response to a loss or trauma.

My goal in this chapter was to show that I have been at the bottom of those valleys. I have experienced the hardships that so many other people have experienced. Loss, pain, and grief are not easy to overcome. I get it. I know it. I have lived it.

I want to give you hope. I want to show you how you can start to heal and recover. I want to show you that your life still has purpose and meaning. That it can still be filled with love. There are so many more peaks out there for you to crest.

Having had this White Light afterlife experience, I can certainly give you hope from a personal understanding of what lies ahead for all of us. There will be a reuniting with loved ones on the other side! There is a chance for healing on this side, no matter your circumstance! Love and forgiveness on this side of the veil give us an understanding of what lies ahead for all of us. Spirit tells us about our free will and gives us hope.

> One free will choice every morning, has the capability to change our life. Anger and vengeance have motive. Love and forgiveness bring peace. *blrd

I want to finish this chapter with the Kindergarten Run. This is something that David and I worked on together. Of course, I got his help from the other side. We worked on this as a team. The Kindergarten Run is a way to help us understand that we can still have a life that includes loved ones that we have lost.

When I was in kindergarten, the other children and I would be picked up every morning by a lady driving a blue station wagon. After we were dropped off at the front door of the facility, the teacher would then take over and start escorting us down this long hallway. First, we would have to go down a small flight of concrete steps that ended at the beginning of the hallway.

Every day as soon as we got to the bottom of the steps at the landing, the same group of boys would take off running down the hallway towards the classroom. Also, every day these same boys would get in trouble for making this sprint towards the doorway of the room. As bad as I wanted to run free with these boys, I did not. I walked with the rest of the children, not wanting to get into trouble.

My heart was telling me to run like the wind. My mind was telling me to behave and adhere to the rules like I was supposed to. Keep this in mind, the turmoil of wanting to, but not doing so. I was doing exactly what society and its rules had taught me.

I want to now make the point of this story. Through our grief and/or loss, once we are ready to start healing, we need to make the effort to do so. We can still have a life with our loved ones on the other side, or even with those on this side, if that is the kind of healing we need. Here is the thing though, we cannot expect them to do all the work. We need to be willing to meet them halfway. In a sense, we need to bypass the societal rules and find our own way.

If we are trying to get signs from our loved ones on the other side, communicate with them, or just feel them in our hearts, we need to do the Kindergarten Run. This can also be used in relationships with those that are still with us here on the earth plane. What we need to do is listen to our heart, not our mind. Letting go and setting our heart free is the lesson to be learned.

Run down that hallway. Meet them halfway. They will be there, but we need to do our part. Listen to your heart and run like the wind. Never mind what you have been taught or what society says you should do. You will be surprised at the results that you will get in doing so.

I will write a lot more about signs and healing in the coming chapters, but I wanted to explain the Kindergarten Run here. Now that we know what it is, I want us to use it at the end of the next chapter. After writing about healing and growing in the coming chapter, I will cue you to do the Kindergarten Run at the end of the next chapter. Run like the wind! Open your heart and let the healing begin!

CHAPTER SIX

• • •

Healing and Living Again

HEALING CAN BE a difficult thing to accomplish. I believe, for the most part, healing comes from within. Though counseling and other forms of therapy are a lot of times needed and effective, I believe these forms of healing simply put into motion things that are already available to us. They are within.

I am a self-healer. I have been through many setbacks in my life but have always relied upon myself for healing. Seeking professional help may be the answer to get one's life back to some normality though. My self-healing, of course, had a lot to do with my White Light experience.

In God's White Light, a person comes away with an understanding of the afterlife. I feel fortunate to have had this experience. It was life changing. God's light heals everything.

Letting go of the past is an important part of healing. It is hard, and at times almost impossible to enjoy the present-day life you are living if the past is still haunting you. Learning to live in the now and letting go of yesterday and tomorrow can certainly help in resetting your life. Spirit shares a message about this with us here.

> *Peace is the understanding of accepting everything as it is.*
> *Peace is knowing you have the capability to change the*
> *future with free will but being able to let go of the past.*
> *blrd

In the last chapter we talked about loss and the grief associated with it. Losing someone close, such as a child, will change your life forever. This *change* that comes with the loss is the part that we must learn to rise above for our own healing.

I understand these losses first-hand, but we need to go on living and rise above. That is what our loved ones on the other side want us to do. I connect to the other side daily, so I know this to be true!

That is what this chapter is meant to address. Rising above the grief and loss of a loved one. I will let Spirit explain, from the other side, ways of looking at things with an eternal perspective. This eternal perspective is love.

Love and forgiveness are the key to peace, happiness, and healing. Using Spirit's understanding of these key ingredients can certainly set our wheels into motion. This will allow us to rise above and heal. Rising above is a form of raising our vibration with love and forgiveness, to conquer pain, loss, and the grief associated with it.

Spirit talks about practicing love and forgiveness in this next lesson. They also talk about letting go of the past.

> *If you are not practicing love and forgiveness, then you*
> *cannot find your peace. Love everyone. Love yourself.*
> *Forgive everyone. Especially forgive yourself. This allows*
> *you to find your peace which is the ultimate reward.*

> *When Jesus spoke of turning the other cheek, he did not mean to let someone continue to harm you. He meant to let things go. Do not get hung up on things that happened in the past. Do not dwell on it. Move on and forgive.* ★blrd

I understand that if you lost a loved one, you may feel like there is nothing to forgive. You may feel that forgiving has nothing to do with the grief that you need to heal from. Getting your heart right is a big part of the healing process, so having forgiveness in your heart does help in any healing process. Spirit explains, in a down to earth way, how having a healthy heart is so important.

> *If you take anger out of your heart and replace it with forgiveness, you will change your life. A healthy heart is a heart without anger. Cardio day takes on a new meaning when you do not have to go to the gym. When you get up in the morning, make it a cardio (heart) day. The more you work on fixing yourself, the more you realize that you have no need to fix anyone else.* ★blrd

Having anger in your heart can impede the healing process dramatically. Always remember, if you have anger in your heart it belongs to you, not to someone else. Letting go of anger brings forgiveness.

> *If you carry anger in your heart, you carry it in your heart. If you carry forgiveness in your heart, you are allowing someone else to lose the anger in their heart. To heal and find happiness, you need to first be happy with yourself.* ★blrd

Accepting yourself as you are and even accepting your circumstances are also a key to healing. Once you understand that you cannot change the past, as bad as it may have been, then you are taking a step forward. This first step might not seem like much, but it is huge. Moving forward is key. Of course, there is a time for grieving and recovery, and everyone's timetable is different. Do what works for you.

You can hate the world, or God Source, all day long for allowing something bad happen to you. This will not change your circumstances. The past is the past. We own it. It will not go away or change. We need to learn a way to live differently. This process takes time.

Another key element of healing and finding peace is perception. I am talking about how we put out to others how we want to be perceived. I believe we get back what we put out. Some people call it karma. If we hate everything in the world, we are asking the world to hate us back. If we send out love, we are asking the world to love us back. This is an important part of the healing process.

> *Gifts are given to make someone feel appreciated, acknowledged, or recognized. They are given to make someone feel good about themselves or to get well. Give generously. Start each day off by giving the most important gift of all. A gift to yourself of acceptance, forgiveness, and love.*
>
> *After doing so, you will be giving gifts out all day long. This will set in motion a day of good energy. This good energy will radiate out to others.* ★blrd

I absolutely love the following story. In it, Spirit gives an example of how children can teach us life lessons, if we are willing to learn. I believe things like anger, jealousy, and hate, are things taught to us by adults as we are growing up. Children, for the most part, have a pure heart. The same kind of heart that souls have on the other side.

Also, Spirit again talks about getting back what we put out in the world. We truly can, over time, receive what we give. To heal, we must find a way to live in the flow of all that is.

I ran into Santa the other day and his bag seemed fuller than usual. I asked him why. He said that he was giving everyone on the planet a 'Magic Boomerang.' He asked me to help him and spread the word.

I agreed, then asked him why the boomerangs were magic. I also thought it was odd that they were shaped like a heart. He told me that when you throw one of the magic boomerangs, it comes back with three words on it. He told me to watch what happens next.

So, Santa had ten children throw the magic boomerangs, then ten adults, and lastly, Santa himself threw one. He then asked me what I learned. I said that every time a child threw it, regardless of their race or gender, it came back with the words, peace, love, and forgiveness on it.

But when the adults threw it, regardless of race or gender, a lot of times it came back with the words, anger, jealousy, and hate on it. I told him that when he threw it, it came back with the same words as the children on it. The words, peace, love, and forgiveness.

I then asked him why his words were in red letters. He told me that he is doing the work of an old friend, and they always put his words in red letters when he spoke. I thanked Santa, then asked him what the boomerangs were called. He said, "Karma." ★blrd

In the following messages from my Spirit Guide, Lida, we are again reminded to let go of the past. He also mentions how karma does affect us.

'Return to sender,' you get back what you send out. ★Lida

> *No matter how hard the world hit you yesterday,*
> *remember that was yesterday. To find freedom in peace,*
> *one must be willing to let go and release.* ★Lida

So far, in this chapter, we have talked about losing anger, having forgiveness and love, and karma. Next, I would like to talk about attitude. Again, this is a part of the change needed in rising above. Changing our attitude can raise our vibration. If we look at things with love instead of anger or hate, it certainly can change our lives. I give an example of this in the following message.

> *As the rooster crows signaling a new dawn every morning,*
> *get up with the attitude of finding your peace through love*
> *and forgiveness. The new day comes with peace. Send back*
> *to it what it gave you, peace and love.* ★blrd

Moving forward with the same type of message, I love how they simply put things into perspective with such ease and elegance. Think hard about this next message. Try to use it in your life every day. Our attitude really does have a lot to do with how we perceive the world and what we expect to get back out of it.

This simple phrase can really impact our lives and help with healing. I believe this phrase, if used, can help us find our peace. I try to remember and use it every day in my life.

> *A man that gets up every morning and looks for something*
> *to disagree with or be angry about, will be successful. A*
> *man that gets up every morning and looks for something*
> *to inspire him or bring him peace, will also be successful.*
> ★blrd

Carrying on with this same theme of attitude and now also learning to let go, I love the following message.

> *To reach the higher vibrational realms, one must let go of the lower vibrations. Always look for the light, not the darkness. A higher vibrational life yields a lot more love.*
> ★ blrd

The previous lessons are about attitude, letting go, and love. Part of letting go involves working on ourselves. Not trying to work on others. We can help others by first helping ourselves. Spirit tells us this in the following message.

> *Give everyone a chance. Do not judge. Let another man make his own journey. Do not try to picture their journey, picture your own journey. Send out light and you will receive light.* ★blrd

In the following story, we are reminded to work on ourselves. Everything starts from within. Just think if we spent as much time trying to make ourselves better instead of trying to make other people the way we want them to be, or vice versa. There is so much wisdom in this lesson.

> *A man, as he is entering heaven, is so excited and happy. He tells God that it is just as he had said it would be. He explains to God how he told others they were wrong, and he was right about God and heaven.*
>
> *Next, the man notices people who are in heaven who did not see things the same way as him. He asks God why he allowed this because he worked so hard to do what his religion had taught him. God says, "Son, everyone's path is different. If a person had to be perfect to get to heaven, you wouldn't be here."*

> *The man told God that he read the Bible, so he was*
> *right, and they were wrong. God replied, "My son, man*
> *wrote the Bible. Man is not perfect. I wish you had put*
> *as much energy into helping people, as you did into telling*
> *them they were wrong. Nonetheless, welcome home son.*
> *Here, you are loved even without perfection. I welcome you*
> *home, just as you are, with unconditional love." ★blrd*

Healing starts the process of living again. They go hand in hand. It truly is the little things that can have a major impact on our life. Practicing these small things in our daily lives can truly open the door to a higher vibrational life of healing. This will lead us to living a full life again.

We can, in no way, shape, or form, worry about what others might think or say about us. There is a way to let go and release ourselves from these thoughts. Let us keep our eye on the ball of ourselves, as we heal OUR hearts.

If someone thinks or says that you should have healed by now and that you have had enough time to sort things out and start living again, how does this affect us? It does not. It only affects us if we allow it to. Here in this next story, is an example of how everyone is different and has their own timetable. To heal ourselves we need to do what is necessary for our healing not what others think our healing should be.

> *The lady at the office told the woman that everyone knew*
> *she had lost a loved one, but they all felt it was time for*
> *her to move on. The woman took her shoes off and handed*
> *them to the lady. The lady said, "I can't wear these. They*
> *are too worn out and faded. Besides, they don't fit." The*
> *woman replied, "Exactly." ★blrd*

As we finish up what Spirit has to say about healing and move into learning to live again, I will give what they say about a forgiving heart, working on our own self, and just simply being ourselves.

> *A free heart is equal to a free soul. Let your heart and soul be free to live. Be kind. Love, live, and laugh, one step at a time. Help others, but do not try to fix them. Let a man work on fixing himself. Live just simply being who you are.* ★blrd

I believe the previous message about simply being who we are can lead us to living a much fuller life. We cannot allow ourselves to be worried about what others think or want us to be. If what we are doing is not hurting anyone, then let us do what inspires us and/or makes us happy. Remember, this is our life and peace, not someone else's.

I love how Spirit keeps things so simple. In this next message, they are simply telling us to be ourselves.

> *Do not try to park in the 'best' parking spot, park in 'your' parking spot.* ★blrd

Releasing from other people's opinions and being who we want to be is so important in living our own life. Here is another quick message about letting go of others' thoughts and being ourselves.

> *Perception can be how others see you. Their perception of you is possibly a reflection of them. Let not what another man thinks cloud your vision. Let another man think as he pleases. Let another man be another man. Understand this and move on.* ★blrd

Accepting and being happy with our lives gives us the ability to live again. We cannot just try to live our new journey.

We also need to be content with it. Simply talking about a new or different kind of life will not make it more fulfilling. Happiness comes with this acceptance.

> *A man cannot just live in the now, he needs to be satisfied with it as well. Be content and release all that was. Releasing and unwinding are a lot like taking a soak in a nice hot bath. You let your guard down and accept your being.* ★blrd

Learning to live again after a life changing event, like the loss of a loved one and/or child, is not easy. When we get to this point of healing and living again, we have done so because we have accepted our situation. We have not forgotten why we are in this new place of our life, nor have we forgotten our loved ones on the other side. We simply have come to an understanding that this is where our journey has brought us.

This new life of ours comes from finding peace, somehow or some way. We move forward in our journey with scars from the past. These scars are reminders of where we have been. We carry them with us forever. They never go away.

Do we want them to go away? I do not think so. This scar that I carry from losing loved ones, including my son, is a reminder of the joy that they brought to my life. I consider myself lucky to have had these loved ones in my life.

With our newfound peace and acceptance, we have learned to simply be. This is so important in our new way of living our lives. Others that have not walked the same paths as we have on our journey may not understand it, but that is okay. They were not meant to understand it, we were.

These life lessons that we have learned have helped in our growth. The loss of these loved ones planted a seed for us. It is our job to nurture and allow this seed to grow into something that is so much bigger than we are.

This wonderful place of what the seed grows into is our new responsibility. It is our new way of living. Our journey may have unexpectantly put this responsibility upon us. We can always think back to where this new growth came from. It came from the seed planted by the loss of a loved one.

Let us honor them by making the best of our situation. This new place we are in is our place of peace. It is a place that we have created to allow what is meant to be to grow and prosper. Spirit gives us an example of this in the following message.

> *Find your peace and you find yourself, along with many answers. You may not receive a message of learning or feel a sense of connection to the Source every time you meditate or connect. You simply are putting yourself into a place of allowing it to happen.* ★blrd

I believe this previous message has the meaning of when you start living a new kind of life, you have done so because you allowed it to happen. Through your grief that came from loss, you started to heal. In this healing, you started to accept and live again. This was done by finding your peace. You have done so by allowing this seed to grow into what was meant to be.

Living in this new place *of the now* means that you have started to release from the past. This does not mean you have forgotten the past. You have simply started to accept it. The scar remains, but it is there to remind us of the seed that our loved one planted.

Once we have gotten to this part of our journey, we have come so far. The valleys were deep. The last peak seems so far away and long ago.

Yet, if we look forward into the new growth of our loved ones' seed, we can see the next peak. It is there for us to crest. For us to get to the top of this next peak on our journey, we must keep a positive attitude. We cannot allow ourselves to be drawn back into the lower vibrations of the last valley.

We understand and know that there will be bad days ahead for us. There will be days when we need to haul heavy loads of water to nurture the new growth of our seed. Some days will be cloudy, but we know this is normal. Letting go and being emotional at times is a good thing.

One of the most important things that I learned from my White Light experience is that if you are not living through your emotions, then you are not fully living. Laughter is good for the soul. But what I learned from God's Light is that you need to live all your emotions.

If you are not willing to shed a tear here and there, you are missing out on so much. Let your emotions run wild. Keep them in check but let them flow. Doing so will also let your heart run free and give your life so much more flow with *all that is.*

Finding a way to stay positive can take some practice. Sometimes we need a routine to help us get something to become a habit. Another way that Spirit teaches us how to stay focused is in the next message.

> *Every time that you wash your hands each day, picture yourself in the White Light. This will help you stay focused and in a positive mindset.* ★blrd

I love this last message. Think about how many times we wash our hands each day. This can obviously give us a routine that creates a habit. This habit will then help us stay focused and positive throughout the day. Doing so will certainly help us keep our eye on the next peak. The peak, of course, that our loved one is leading us to.

As we start wrapping up this chapter, I want to briefly discuss growth. This growth is what we have obtained from learning to live again and healing. We have done so after going through our grief, due to our own personal loss.

This growth comes not only from staying positive, healing, and living again, but it also comes from that very seed that our loved one planted for us in our loss of them. This is now our journey. We are now living again. Doesn't it feel wonderful?

Staying neutral, when it comes to dealing with others, can help us so much in our growth. By not judging others and accepting them as they are, we have grown. This is in our energy field around us. We cannot let others invade our positive space with their negative energy.

Our new life that we have grown into through loss, grief, healing, and staying positive, has got us to where we are. We cannot allow ourselves to be drawn back into the last valley from someone else's thoughts.

> *A man can learn and grow more a lot of times from a neutral position. Better decisions can be made by not first judging what is being said by someone while they are saying it. First, understand why they are saying it, then do not let their words plant seeds of anger, let them plant seeds of understanding. Be willing to learn from others, not be insulted by them.* ★blrd

We have gotten to this healing place of peace that we now reside in from hard work. We have learned to accept, forgive, heal, live again, and stay positive. We now realize that we are not perfect and are not going to be perfect.

Achieving happiness equals finding peace. This peace was already in our heart, we just had to learn to live again to find it. Replacing anger with love and forgiveness has given us this new lease on life. Accepting ourselves as we are has given us this freedom in our heart. This peace that we have gained from our spiritual growth has no monetary value, but it is priceless!

The following is a message about spiritual growth. The same kind of growth that we have obtained from working hard at living again.

True spiritual growth has happened when you-
No longer meditate, you connect.
No longer try to make things happen, you let them happen.
No longer expect, you accept.
No longer try to be as others want you to be, you become who you are.
No longer carry anger, you carry love and forgiveness.
No longer judge others, you respect them.
No longer look outwardly to find your peace, you look within.
No longer live by religious rules, you follow your heart.
No longer value material things, you use them like tools.
No longer have ego, you have spiritual growth. *blrd

Closing out this chapter, I now invite you to join me. With all that we have learned in this chapter about healing, living again, staying positive and growing, we can now come together as we head into the next chapter about signs. These signs from loved ones on the other side are available to all of us if we are willing to meet them halfway. Look ahead to the next peak.

The peak that was made possible from the seed planted by our loved one.

So now, I invite you to join me! Run with me down that hallway! Let your heart and emotions run wild! Run like the wind! Be free and enjoy this new life you are living! Here we go, let us do this together because we are never alone on our journey! Let us do the Kindergarten Run!

CHAPTER SEVEN

* * *

Signs from the Other Side

WHEN I USE the word *signs*, I am talking about things that Spirit does to get our attention. These signs are a way for them to let us know that they are in our lives. This also shows that Spirit has the capability to live in both worlds at the same time. The reason for this, I believe, is because there is no separation. Both worlds are part of the one consciousness that I call God.

Signs can be given to us by any being on the other side. They can come from lost loved ones, Spirit Guides, Holy Ones, angels, Jesus, and God. These usually are just little nudges, but once recognized, hit us right smack in the face.

There are many reasons a soul from the other side may send us signs. It may be when we are going through hard times, or there is an important event in our life. We can also get these signs when they just want to say hello and let us know they are still in our lives.

Always remember that spirits like to have fun too. It is not like they sit on the other side and meditate and stay in a continuous serious mood. Spirits like to goof off and have recreational time as well.

These souls just live at a higher vibration than us. The key word here being *live*. This is because they are still alive. They just do not have the burden of carrying around these bulky bodies anymore, lol. Spirits are still having a life on the other side. We will get into this a lot more in the coming chapters.

Many times, after someone loses a loved one, they talk about all the signs they got from that person right after their crossing over to the other side. I believe this is because we are in a state of higher awareness. In our period of grieving, we have blocked out most of the rest of the world.

This is in line with what I wrote about earlier in chapter five. As we are in this state of shock and grief, we block out things that we used to think were important, but now realize are not. In doing so, we open our awareness at the soul level.

We, at that point, are living from the heart, not the ego. This allows us to see things differently, things that a lot of times we would not otherwise pick up on. Our bond with these loved ones is never broken at the soul (heart) level.

An acronym that I like to use when it comes to *signs* is UFOOS. This stands for–

> Unidentifiable
> Feelings
> Oddities
> Odors or
> Sights

Of course, the unidentifiable part is in relation to your environment. For instance, if you smell cigar smoke that smells like your dad's and you are at a bar, then it probably is not your dad giving you a sign. But if you smell that cigar smoke and you are at church, it more than likely is your dad saying hello.

When an incident like this happens, look around and be aware. Your dad's favorite hymnal may be being sang by the choir. Or you might be sitting behind someone that has the same name as him. There can be many other secondary signs to finish the message. These secondary signs are there to further validate the sign given to you by Spirit.

I like to say when you get one of these UFOOS, freeze the situation in your mind. If you do not have the time then, go back to that space/time later and see if there was another message for you in the environment that it happened. You can do this in your mind.

First, go back to that space/time, then expand the environment in your mind, and go into it. Once you are back into that specific space/time and environment, then you might recognize things that you did not pick up on when it happened.

There are so many ways to receive signs. They can be in song lyrics, movies, license plates, billboards, street signs, numbers, electronic signs, birds, feathers, coins, etc. This list goes on and on. Once you do start recognizing signs, then you will notice that a lot of times it is the same sign with the same soul.

For instance, I know that when I find a dime, it is my dad sending the sign. I then start to look around for things that would resonate with him and/or me. If I see a penny, it is my mother-in-law. I also know that my first wife sends me signs from the era that we were together.

But most importantly, I know that my son, David, uses hands to get my attention. He does this because I have a plaster of Paris handprint of his. I also get a lot of signs through song lyrics and music.

It is fun to do, once you recognize that it is going on. Sometimes they give you hints and kind of lead you on a scavenger hunt. Their personality and humor can also be a part of this wondrous event.

In these types of signs, stories, and happenings, we then realize it was worth our effort to heal and live again. Our loved ones from the other side are a part of our healing. These signs are sent to assure us that they are still alive and doing well. The next message is something I was told about getting signs.

> *Your spiritual awareness is like a sensor or motion detector.*
> *It is also like the little icon on your smart phone or laptop,*
> *showing how good your Wi-Fi connection is. The signal*
> *is always there, it just depends on how good you are*
> *receiving it.*
>
> *Go to your spiritual settings (your heart) and turn on*
> *the connect/accept button. This will enable all that is (the*
> *signal) to be received. When this mechanism needs charged,*
> *simply go to your place of peace. Here, the charging will*
> *happen while sitting in the silence.* ★blrd

Here is another quick message about sending signs.

> *Just like recessed lighting, you may not see us, but we are*
> *there. We will always shine down on you. You do not have*
> *to see the source, just know that it is there.* ★blrd

I love the following lesson that Spirit gives us about always being there for us and how developing our own awareness will help us see more signs.

> *We are like lifeguards watching over people on earth. We*
> *keep an eye and ear on them. We blow our whistle when*
> *trying to get their attention. Most people are too caught*

up in their material lives to notice all the beauty and light
surrounding them.

Take time to pause and be aware. You will be surprised
at what you will see, learn, and pick up on. We are still
together. Feel us. Be with us. We are love. ★Reece

I got this last lesson from Reece in July of 2019. Of course, Reece, is one of my Spirit Guides. When he gave me this message, he was in the palace. The same place that I wrote about in chapter four. Sometimes I do call the palace, the *palace of light*. My son, David, and my Guide, Lida, were also there. They really got a kick out of this message and applauded Reece for it.

It did not even register with me when I jotted this message from Reece down in my journal that he was a swimmer while here on earth. I knew that, but I did not realize he used this synchronicity until I put it here in this book. I love that. This just goes to show that souls are still alive and well. It also shows that they use things that not only resonate with our lives when giving lessons, but also things that resonate with theirs as well.

I will mention that David and Reece helped me come up with the acronym of UFOOS. They were making light of it and saying how they liked the 'OOS' part of it. They were basically trying to be funny, so we all had a good laugh. Hey, what was I supposed to do when two spirits were teaming up on me, lol?

A sign that I like to talk about is one that happened with my wife. She was at the funeral home when it happened. Her mother had just crossed over to the other side. She was sitting in a room waiting for the representative of the funeral home to start helping make the arrangements for her mother.

As she sat there, she looked over at and through a small octagonal window. A red cardinal landed on the edge of the small windowsill. Not only did the cardinal stop and look at her, it also pecked on the window! I love this story. Right after her mother crossed over, she found a way to let her daughter know that she was still with her and doing fine.

Next, I will share a story that Spirit gave me. In this story, they are simply pointing out that people here on earth need to learn how to open themselves up to receive signs. They also make the point that souls on the other side need to learn how to send them as well. Just like in our Kindergarten Run, both sides need to be willing to adjust and make changes so that this connection is possible. I love their creativity in this message.

> *The man had not been away from his house long. As he and a friend got to his home, they both noticed that the man's wife was crying. The friend asked the man why she was crying. The man said, "We just don't see things the same way these days." The friend shook his head and said that he understood.*
>
> *He then asked the man if he had tried to reach out to her. The man said, "Yes, I have, but she just isn't the same person anymore." His friend told him that he should try something different.*
>
> *Listening to his friend, the man put his and his wife's favorite song on the radio. As his wife heard the song start to play, she noticed that the radio was unplugged. Her tears of sadness turned into tears of joy, as the man and his friend happily walked back into the light.* ★blrd

As I mentioned earlier in the book, I am in a gratitude group with other people who have lost children. We communicate with each other almost daily. One day, I told them that I had asked David for a sign. After doing so, I went on with the regular routine of my day not thinking much about it.

When I got home from work, my granddaughter was there visiting. She had the television on and started watching a children's show. On the screen of the television were numerous hands. They were part of the show. A show, I might add, that I had never seen her watch before that day.

The screen was covered with hands. I got my sign. *Hands* are one of my signs from David. Remember the plaster of Paris hand print I have of his? Another smack in the face. I love getting hit like that, lol.

This last story had an example of how you can ask for signs. They do not always have to show up unexpectedly. If you do ask for a sign from a guide or loved one, a general rule I use is to ask for it in the next forty-eight hours. I do this because if you ask for a specific sign and get it two weeks later, it probably is not a sign.

Another point here in this story is that since time is different on the other side, maybe David knew that my granddaughter would be watching that show on television. Having that knowledge in advance, he could have put the thought of me asking for a hand sign into my mind. I believe this, more than likely, happens quite often.

Signs and messages are always there. Practice raising your awareness and you will be amazed at what you will start to see and/or get.

As we move into the last part of this book, *the other side*, I am so excited to share with you what Spirit has to say. Keep your awareness open for any UFOOS!

PART III

• • •

The Other Side

CHAPTER EIGHT

. . .

What Happens During and After Crossing Over to the Other Side?

PART THREE OF this book has so much information about the entire topic of the afterlife. I will write about cross over and what happens at that point and beyond. What souls do on the other side and how things work there, will also be discussed. I will give all aspects of what Spirit has taught me about the other side. This will also include what it is like there and some wonderful wisdom that has been shared with me.

As we go through this part of the book, keep in mind all the topics from the first two parts. The topics in those two parts were written for a reason. That reason was so that you would understand this part of the book.

In this part, when Spirit Guides, souls, Guardian Angels, and all other spirits are discussed, then you will already have an understanding to what my, and Spirit's, writings are about. This will include the Holy Ones and God-ness, as well.

When I write about the temple and palace, try to picture in your mind that you are there and sharing in these parts of the story. Let yourself get lost in the world of the other side as we go there. Most of the stories and information in this last part of the book were given to me by Spirit.

The place of peace will also be referenced to in this part of the book. When they talk about this wonderful place, you will know how to relate to that story or message. Keep all the aforementioned information in mind as we learn from Spirit. Part three will guide you into a wonderful learning experience.

As I mentioned earlier, my White Light experience gave me the gift of understanding what it felt like on the other side. It did not show me details of what it is like there. Now I have the privilege of sharing those details that Spirit has so lovingly given to me. It is time to let them really talk. So that is what I am going to do. Again, they have so much to say.

What happens at cross over? That truly is a great question and may be one of the most thought of questions there is when discussing the subject of death. Of course, only the body dies, not the soul. Spirit has given me guidance on this subject, as well as answering some questions I directed to them.

Right before crossing over to the other side, there are beings of light that are sent to assist in the process. A lot of people call them angels. Usually there are two, but the number can vary a little. There will also be loved ones there to greet us as we embark on this part of our journey.

If you are in a hospital, at home, or in an accident, it does not matter. These beings will be there. This is because it is all a part of the plan. A plan of the soul's journey. The journey that was set into motion years ago.

When my mother-in-law was in the process of crossing over, she had been in the hospital hanging on to her earth life for several days. I never miss a day of connecting. Every day at the hospital I would go into this small meditation/prayer room that was available. Here, I could make my connection and not disturb anyone or interfere with what was going on at the time.

On the last day of her earth life, I was in the meditation/prayer room clearing my mind. As I sat there, two beings of light appeared next to me on a bench. They let me know, telepathically, that it was time for my mother-in-law to cross over. I immediately got up and went into her hospital room and joined my wife and the rest of her family.

Within ten minutes of me entering her room, she started to take her last breaths. The two beings of light (angels) had summoned me right before the event happened. I did not mention this to the family, at that point, but did later. I did not feel it was appropriate at the time.

My mother-in-law was then free to take the next step in her journey as she was being welcomed by two angels, her husband, and other loved ones. She held on until that specific day for a reason. It was, my wife, her daughter's birthday!

I know in my heart that she did that intentionally. What a beautiful gift she gave to her daughter at the very end. It was totally in her character. She always gave with all her heart.

So yes, there are souls and angels present at our time of cross over. They are there to assist and aid so that the soul crossing over is never alone. The souls crossing over are welcomed with love. Spirit told me something that I believe is just wonderful. As I said earlier, I will let them do a lot of the talking in this part of the book. So here it is.

As one starts the process of crossing over, there is a time period that is, well, just wondrous. This is a time that the soul gets to still be in the material world but is also in the spirit world. They literally get to have both worlds at the

> *same time. In this state, they are letting go of one world but being called home by another. They instantly understand what is going on and feel the love of 'all that is.' ★blrd*

Here is what my son, David, told me about crossing over. Of course, he did this from the other side in one of my connections. Part of it reminds me of the Kindergarten Run. I love how he had to decide to meet his mother halfway. I believe this is where the seed for the Kindergarten Run was planted.

> *I was in both worlds at the same time. I could see mommy, but she was off a short distance coming towards me. She was keeping me comforted until it was time to go with her. She kept telling me how much you and everyone else loved me here. During this time, there was no physical pain. I had already left my physical body. My energy was in you.*
>
> *I could see mommy in the mist and light. When it was time to go, she came closer, but I had to go towards her. I had to make that decision. Mommy and the light welcomed me. She held my hand and that is when I became pure energy. That is when we transitioned together into the light, energy, and love.*
>
> *Daddy it was wondrous. We spent some time together before we went to our own life reviews, but our energies never really separated. After the review, I could hear a humming. It was a vibration of all that is. It was the God-ness. ★David*

Here, my son, David gives a wonderful example of what can happen at cross over. I say this because I am sure that not all cross overs are the same. This is simply my son's story. Just like anything else, everyone's journey is different. I found a lot of comfort in his message.

Next, Lida talks about crossing over. I love how he explains what starts to happen after going into the light. The wonder of it all is just beautiful.

> *When souls cross over, they go into the light. They are greeted by angels and loved ones. Next, they go to the palace of light and do several personal soul reviews including a life review. They then are reunited with loved ones. The soul gets to spend time together with loved ones, like a reunion.*
>
> *After this period of reuniting, the soul then starts to settle in and start working on what they need to learn. This helps in their soul growth. Some of this learning can be a healing. It depends on what the soul needs. ★Lida*

I love how in this previous message from Lida, he explains what starts to happen after going into the light.

Another story just fell into my lap this morning. It came from my Guardian Angel, Athena. I mentioned her in chapter four. She was in the palace with me and helped in my mock life review, while I was in trance at work. I had not heard from her since that time last year. This just shows how involved and connected they are to our lives. She obviously had to know that I was going to write this chapter today about crossing over.

To help you understand her story, I will fill you in on some background information. When I was five years old, I had a tumor removed. In doing so, they had to remove my eye. I was then fitted with a prosthetic eye. I was in kindergarten at the time. Hmmm…. Maybe another element of the Kindergarten Run. I love how things just seem to unfold and flow together when we let the power of *all that is* run free.

> *I was with you at the time of your eye operation. I held your hand and we walked together. A child never goes*

through these types of situations alone. There are always souls from the other side gathered and making the soul connection, even if the soul does not cross over.

They are being given comfort, love, and presence in these situations. When a child is sick and nearing the end of his life cycle, they are already being comforted by those on the other side. At that point, the soul has the choice to cross over or take some more time. ★Athena

Another subject that Athena addressed, this same morning, was what can happen when a person lays sick or is getting close to crossing over. I would think that this would resonate with a lot of people when she talks about strange situations. What she says, I believe, will give a lot of these people comfort.

As a person lays sick or in some way is nearing the end of their life cycle, their soul can start to reach out to people before they cross over. There can be odd situations where people involved with the dying person have something happen that they do not understand. It will usually be something very profound and attention getting.

This is where the soul is already starting to work 'deeds of love.' They are doing so even before they shed their body. Understand that that is all they are doing, shedding the body. Only the body is lost, not the soul.

When a child crosses over, there can also be child guides there who have passed from similar circumstances. They can be called upon if needed. Children do not cross over alone. They always have someone there to walk into the White Light of Love with them. ★Athena

There, of course, are many different scenarios when crossing over. As the body dies, the soul is in both worlds. It is in an energy field that surrounds the area on this side of the veil. This is where the magic of being in both worlds takes place. Then the soul is aided by angels as they reunite with their loved ones. They then go into the light.

Next, they start going through soul reviews and a life review. There can be many different elements to this part of the journey. Every soul is unique, even though they are all a part of the oneness. There can be many learning and healing experiences that the soul may go through. It is all done in love and with a welcoming home.

A lot of people want to know who goes to the other side. Everyone goes to the other side. Remember, we are all a part of this one consciousness that I call God. I learned from my White Light experience just how much love is shared on the other side. If you want one word to sum up the other side, here it is, LOVE.

There can be differences though, for those who cross over. Not every soul gets to stay in the soul warming love and light of God. God does love everybody and everything, but there is a place in God's light for everyone. Some may just be where the light is not as bright or warm. I will write more about this after making the next point.

The following message speaks of several things that we just discussed. I love how simple and plain they make things. Maybe they just do it so an average guy like me can understand it, lol.

> *When you go into the White Light, you are healthy and healed right away. If you have been told that your loved one is healing in a hospital on the other side, they very well may be getting healing of the soul. But, make no mistake, you are healed and healthy instantly. You are met with love, compassion, and understanding.* ★blrd

In the last message, they mention a healing of the soul. They say that souls are instantly healed and healthy. The process of healing and raising the vibration of the soul is what is being explained.

This healing of the soul area is a place in the palace of light. This is where the Holy Ones reside, and life reviews and other items of learning are also given. Here is what they had to say about this area. I will tell this story in first person so that you can live it while reading it.

> *There is a medical room in the palace of light. This is where the White Light and healing power of high beings of light, like Jesus, is used. It is used to heal the soul and get rid of any negative energies.*
>
> *The soul still needs to learn its lessons from its recent trip, but this is done to make the soul whole again. This healing of the soul allows the soul to move forward and learn its lessons. Souls of low or no light will not be made whole again at this point.*

Next, Spirit speaks about souls that people here on earth would say had problems or circumstances. It is not our job to judge these people. They are on their own journey. Let us focus on our own.

> *People who took their own lives, had addiction problems, etc., go to the other side just like everyone else. These deaths are not a reason the soul would be kept away from the light. God loves everyone.* ★blrd

So yes, as I said earlier, everyone goes to the other side. Souls who had addictions or took their own life are greeted warmly into God's light. They are just like any other soul that crosses over. These souls may not have lived perfectly, but when it comes down to it, who does?

People who cross into the light with lower vibrations generally have a different path after their life review process. I am talking about people who did bad deeds here on earth. When I say bad deeds, I am not talking about getting traffic tickets, cheating on your spouse, experimenting with drugs, or other so-called bad things. I am talking about bad crimes against humanity, or evil things.

These souls are welcomed into the light like everyone else, but they may soon find themselves in a much dimmer and less warm atmosphere. They cross over just like everyone else, but their soul growth has a lot of catching up to do with others. God takes them in. He allows them to see the light and progress towards higher vibrations.

Next, Spirit talks about the empty space that these souls of low light live in. This is a great example of what happens to people who do bad or evil things. Again, God always gives the chance to grow and love, but souls need to be willing to do so.

There is a room in the palace of light that is down the hallway and on the left. It is past the life review room. This is a place of lessons and learning from lower vibrational deeds. This is a place that souls of lower light go to figure it out and learn their lessons. It is a place of low light, slow vibration, and empty space.

Souls are not being punished there. They are learning lessons and being nourished with love to help raise their vibration. These souls are trapped in their own bad energy until they learn to allow the light of love into their existence. They pace back and forth in their own negative energy until they have seen the light.

As always, they are given love. How long it takes them to allow this love can take some time. People of bad deeds of the lowest nature can be caught up in their own negative energy for eons. Negative energies are feeling their

> *own low vibrations in this area of low light until they are*
> *willing to allow the light of all that is in.* ★blrd

Wow! I found this information to be very enlightening. I can just picture, in my mind, these low vibration souls pacing back and forth in their own negative energy in an empty space. But I also love how they are not given up on. They are sent the love and light of God. These souls need to make the decision to accept it.

I do not believe in hell, as it is recognized by a lot of people. I believe hell only exists on earth. This hell on earth is caused by having an unforgiving and angry heart. An angry heart will cause the soul to burn while here on earth. I believe everyone is given God's love, but some receive it in a different way than others. God gives souls the chance to respond to the love that is given. Here is one thing Spirit has to say about this subject.

> *God does not punish those of bad deeds who reside in the*
> *darkness. Rather, he takes that lifeless, low vibration, dark*
> *matter and tries to make and mold something out of it.*
> *God, over time, turns this lifeless dark matter into light.*
> *God loves everyone. If a soul wants to go from darkness*
> *to light, they need to be willing to make that soul growth*
> *adjustment of love and kindness.* ★blrd

In this previous message, I cannot help but think about the Biblical story of God taking lifeless dark matter and forming the earth and mankind. This message just blows me away! It truly does show the love and light of God and how it can overpower the darkness that tries to get in! Light always overcomes darkness. In this story, Spirit spoke of how God creates light out of darkness. Again, Wow!

I believe the soul reincarnates over and over to learn lessons here on earth. Sometimes souls are put into situations to learn a lesson from a different perspective than they had in a previous life. This can give a soul a chance to see how what they did in a previous life affected those around them. Here, they talk about this and the environment of one's journey.

> *Sometimes souls do not act accordingly. They do bad things here on earth. They do not respond to the purpose of this carnation of their journey. This can cause them to end up in the less lit and less warm light of God. Environment can cause some of these issues.*
>
> *A soul may have to live a life on the other side of the coin from when they did bad deeds. This way they can learn what their bad deeds did in affecting those around them. They may need to live in a different environment. That way they can learn from their mistakes and grow as a soul.*
>
> *Circumstances and environment have a lot to do with life on earth. These are opportunities of growth for a soul. The environment can be better or worse, depending on what the soul needs. It is a perspective of life that gives opportunity for learning.* *blrd

With all the previous messages and teaching from Spirit about what happens to souls of lower light, after crossing over, there is always hope. God always gives hope and love. In the next message, they show how the light is there for those willing to adjust.

> *Souls of low light are welcomed to the other side with love, but their vibration keeps them from attuning to the light of God. They must first deal with what they have done, which can take a long time. They then start to raise their*

vibration. Their vibration relates to their love, compassion, caring, and kindness. Souls of no light have little of these characteristics.

God loves all, but that does not mean a soul's vibration is high enough to stand in his love and light. To raise their vibration, a soul needs to learn how to have these characteristics of love, compassion, and caring. This is so important. ★blrd

In all this information from Spirit, we see that everyone does cross over to the other side. God welcomes all, with love, to be a part of his oneness. We are sent to earth, as a soul, to learn life lessons. Spirit now speaks about this subject.

God does not create perfect individuals. He knows we are not perfect. That is why we are here on earth, to learn these life lessons that allow the soul to grow. Everyone is different in their own imperfect way. If everyone were perfect, there would be no need to come here to learn and grow. God simply gives us opportunities to give and receive love. ★blrd

To sum up this chapter, we have learned that all people cross over to the other side. They are healed from all illness, handicaps, addictions, and other vices, instantly in the White Light of God. In this light, they are aided by angels and reunited with loved ones. There is no fear, only love.

They then go to learn soul lessons and have a life review in the palace of light. This can take some time depending on each individual soul's own personal journey. In the palace, healing of the soul takes place. Holy Ones and beings of high light reside there and aide in the raising of vibration.

Souls of no light have a lot of learning and lessons to learn before they can leave the space where they are trapped. This space is empty and void of most light. It is their own energy that they are trapped in. It is a sense of learning what they did to others and feeling these bad deeds in their own environment. They are experiencing what they did to others.

God loves everyone and everything. He takes these dark souls and tries to form them into light. How long it takes depends on the soul itself. God then allows *all that is* to flow through everything in the oneness of love. This love is God.

After souls are finished with their life review and soul lessons in the palace, they then again reunite with their loved ones. The wonder of it all now starts to happen, and they flow in synchronicity with the love of God. They now move forward to the next part of their journey. It is like they have checked in at their destination.

They now get to live in harmony, balance, peace, and love. This is done in the City of Light. The City of Light, sits right outside the palace. Here, the bonding of souls takes place. It is like a reawakening for the soul at this point because there never really was any separation to start with.

The soul is now free to do what is necessary for their growth. They have unlimited abilities and growth opportunities. They have gone home. The soul is now at one with *all that is*. The soul is now only love. I know this because I have felt it and I have been there!

In the next chapter, Spirit tells us what it is like on the other side. I want to share one story of mine that I got while connecting. It is a story about the soul. I thought it fitting to tell it here. Hopefully, it will answer some questions for someone out there reading this book.

> *I know that dogs, cats, horses, and other animals have souls. I know this because I have had them step forward in readings for my sitters. I do not believe that things such as trees have souls. They are also living things, but I have*

never had a tree step forward in a reading and say, "Hey, remember me?"

But, that said, I have had specific trees show up in readings. So maybe they are showing that their presence of life was connected to that specific person or people that lived there. Maybe this is a sign from a living creature reaching out and saying, "I am a part of the one consciousness. The oneness of God. Remember me?"

CHAPTER NINE

• • •

What is it Like on the Other Side?

IN THIS CHAPTER, I can truly give my personal story of the other side. I can do this because of my afterlife experience. I do know what it feels like on the other side. It is a place of peace and love.

I will not go into all the details of this experience because I wrote about it in my first book, FIFTY YEARS OF SILENCE NO MORE. I do need to relate this story to help with the understanding of what it is like on the other side. Spirit again will speak for themselves. This is what they have asked to do.

I will never forget what happened as I was led through my afterlife experience by Wilma. As I mentioned earlier in the book, Wilma is a family friend on the other side. During this afterlife experience, as I stood face to face with her, she told me telepathically that they wanted me to know what it felt like there. This is an experience that I will never forget.

I felt the pure love and light of God running throughout my entire body. There is not anything negative in your existence.

There is only love. You understand, telepathically, that God is not a person. He is the essence of *all that is*. God's energy pulsated through my body as an overwhelming presence of love. I understood right then and there that God is only love!

The White Light that I was standing in is what sent this feeling of love and peace to me. The light was bright but not blinding bright. It had a warming sense to it. The White Light warmed my soul. It was incredible and I feel fortunate to have had the privilege to stand in it. The loving energy of God raised my vibration so much that it felt like I was going to start floating.

As you are in the White Light of God, you are given the ability to understand a million thoughts at once. You can process and accept all these things smoothly and with a flow of understanding. You only feel love. Also, there is no way you can send out anything but love. There is only positive vibration. God's light is an all healing energy. There is no way anything can be unhealed or unloving in this environment.

I can tell you that your loved ones on the other side are feeling nothing but love. They share in an environment so full of peace, love, and light, that it is impossible to explain or make someone understand that has not been there. It is pure love. It is pure joy and happiness. It is *all that is*.

When you are on the other side, you have no worries. Your mind is at ease. It is not going this way and that way. It is at peace. You get an understanding of balance and peace, along with love. A sense of knowing is guiding you.

Your heart is free, and you let God's love guide you with this sense of knowing that is there in your heart. You are in tune with everything. This is peace. The kind of peace that I have worked on so diligently on this side of the veil to obtain.

Everything is in balance on the other side. Souls on the

other side walk in this balance. It comes with an understanding of walking in the peace. The kind of qualities that I described in the previous paragraphs. Their existence is a steady, balanced stride. They walk in the balance of this knowing, understanding, love, and peace.

Spirit gave me a couple examples of this balance, using sketches. The first sketch is a five-pointed star. They told me that the top point represents the afterlife (heaven) and higher self. The bottom two points represent earth. In the middle, these two points represent the balance of the soul and the ego between heaven and earth.

I thought this was just an amazing, yet simple, way of illustrating how there is a delicate balance of the soul and body. This balance is what a soul walks in on the other side. It is never unbalanced like it can be here on earth. The balance on the other side is continuous and everlasting.

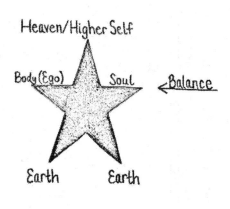

Star

The second sketch uses a cross to make the same point. In my opinion, Spirit is saying to open your mind and you can see things in a different light. We recognize the cross as being a symbol for the crucifixion of Jesus. Maybe it can also be used to show the delicate balance between heaven and earth.

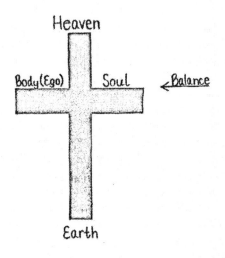

Cross

Our higher self is our soul that is on the other side. Spirits have no limits. The higher self is what we are connected to on the other side. It is the main part of our soul that stays in the afterlife. Our soul here on earth is connected to our higher self at the soul level. Many different parts of the soul can operate in different places at the same time. This is because of the soul's limitlessness.

For instance, you might feel like you felt the presence of your lost child at ten in the morning on Thursday. At the same time and day, your spouse has a reading with a psychic medium and your lost child also communicates with them. This is an example of how the soul is limitless and can be at more than one place at a time. The are no boundaries on the other side.

There is no separation. The soul is at one with all that is. This connectedness allows for the love and balance to flow. We are always connected to our higher self whether we realize it or not. I love how Spirit explains this in the following message.

> *You are connected to your higher self while here on earth. Of course, it is your soul. This, along with your guides, is your sense of knowing and intuition. It is like an old friend that has been with you your entire life. The inner presence that you have felt is your higher self (soul).*
>
> *This is what gives you balance here on earth. It is this connection that can help you find peace. The balance of your higher self gives peace. This peace comes through your heart.* *blrd

I posed a couple of questions to my guides. I wanted to know if a soul can be living and present in more than one life (body) at a time. Also, I wanted to know if someone, such as a medium, can talk with the soul on the other side even though it has already reincarnated and started living an earth life again. I simply wanted to know if these types of incidents can occur. Here is what they, quickly and in short, replied.

> *Yes, there is no separation. We can pick up on the vibrations of your questions or connections even though we are in another body. Our higher self remains the constant. It is all knowing and aware.* *blrd

I will continue by letting Spirit explain more about the soul. In this next message, I love how they explain how everything is within. You sometimes just need to go deep inside your heart.

> *Your higher self allows you to see other aspects and opportunities throughout your life. These opportunities*

were not there by chance. They were put there for a reason. Going to your higher self is a knowing and understanding that things are as they are supposed to be.

Once you find this place, you can then begin to expand your consciousness. You are in a place of acceptance and knowing. There are no expectations here, only a sense of IS. Once you get to the place of IS, you can then grow spiritually. ★blrd

Spirit's next story is about the benefit of connecting to the higher self. I love how Spirit tried to explain this to me. Here, Lida and Reece take me to what they called the re-creation room in the palace. This is how I journaled what they tried to explain.

I see stars and the universe. It is God's creation, but it is nothing more than a thought. There are other universes, it seems. Everything on this side is nothing more than thought. The higher self knows and understands this.

Connecting to your own higher self will bring you to a complete understanding. It is where you can understand one million different things at once. Just like in the White Light. Going to your higher self puts you back in the White Light. The creation story is also about the soul evolving and growing. ★Lida and Reece

In this sketch, Spirit explains how the self and higher self, come together at the higher vibrations. This is a representation of the soul meeting back up with the higher self in the afterlife. I love how they used a pyramid to symbolize this.

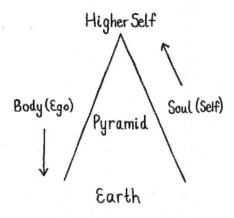

Pyramid

In the last part of this chapter, Spirit will continue to explain more about the other side. In this next message, they let us know how new souls arriving on the other side feel about their newfound situation. Also, what they may bring with them.

> *There is a sense of peace. They are in a transitional period. They understand the love and light. Souls know right away that they have gone home. They are now a part of the higher consciousness and God-ness.*
>
> *They arrive with luggage full of their rights and wrongs. This luggage is opened at their life review and gone through. On their departure of the life review, the luggage in no longer needed. There is only peace and love.* ★blrd

Another question I asked was how they knew when someone was calling on them from earth. I knew how it worked from our side, since I give mediumship readings. I wanted to know how it worked from their side. Here is what they told me.

> *Our souls connect on earth, whether we realize it or not.*
> *As we are with each other on earth we pick up on this*
> *vibrational calling card. It is like a phone number or beacon.*
> *When that number is sent out from earth, we recognize*
> *it and therefore are alerted. Also, when a medium sends*
> *out a signal to a soul, they can pick up on our vibration as*
> *we respond to their signal or beacon.* ★blrd

The last thing I want to mention is an operational aspect of how the other side works. I am talking about the different levels of vibration. Souls like Jesus and other Holy Ones, Saints, and Enlightened Ones vibrate at a high level. Most souls do not vibrate that high. Though all souls do live together in perfect harmony on the other side.

Some souls rise to the level of guide. Other souls go to the level of high light, like angels. There are also what I like to call elders, or gatekeepers. Beings like my guide, Lida, are elders. These elders are also masters, and teachers. There are different levels of vibration and light. There are souls that are just souls and continue with their journey of learning and growth. Here is what Spirit says about this subject.

> *There are different levels of vibration, but they are not just*
> *levels of development, like guides, angels, etc. Sometimes*
> *you can just fit into these levels from your vibration alone.*
> *Thus, like being on the same vibrational level as an*
> *angel does not mean that you need to be an angel. You can*
> *be there due to your vibration. Some souls are not meant*
> *to be anything but at the level of being a soul, but their*
> *vibration might take them to a high level in the light.* ★blrd

To sum up this chapter, we have learned that souls live in a balanced world of pure love. They live with an understanding and knowing that all is as it is supposed to be. Spirit showed us how the soul reincarnates on earth as part of its journey. This part of the journey is representing the delicate balance between heaven and earth.

We are always connected to our higher self. This soul level connection, at the heart, guides us in our daily lives. We are never alone. There is no separation. There is only love.

Souls pick up on our messages (signals) with their dialed in awareness. The White Light of God has different vibrational levels. Souls are free and limitless. They have the capability to shine in the high vibrations with the Masters, and Holy Ones, such as Jesus.

CHAPTER TEN

· · ·

Spirit Works

AS WE CONTINUE learning about the other side, Spirit will explain several more topics. They will explain how new energies are made. Spirit will tell what they can accomplish from the other side. They will also talk about how things work there.

One might wonder how new souls are created. Of course, they are created with the love and light of God. But, if souls are energies of light with limitless abilities, where does that new energy come from?

Using numerology, some souls are said to be new, or younger souls. Some are said to be older, wiser souls. There are even some souls said to be masters, or the oldest of souls. So, the question is, where does this new energy come from when a new (young) soul is created?

To answer that, I again say, this new energy comes from the Source, God, the creator. The Source is limitless. It is the creator of all light. But, again, where does this energy come from? I think that Spirit explains very well how new energies or souls are created in these next messages.

> *Making love on the other side, literally is 'making' love. New energies are made for new souls. Some souls are old, and some are young. New, or the youngest souls, are created by souls making this new love. God's love and light are limitless, just as each soul is.*
>
> *When beings of the highest light start vibrating at these limitless levels, part of their energy is recycled back into the light. This extra high vibrational love and light become part of the light. It is then used in the creation of new souls.*
>
> *Also, when these beings vibrate at the level of the very highest light, part of that energy stays in the light and merges with the God-ness.* ★David

These last messages are saying that the new energies are coming from the unlimited circle of light and life of the God Source. This Source is the creator of *all that is.* Everything circulates and recycles through the Source.

I believe that our soul reincarnates and comes back to earth to learn different life lessons on each trip. This gives the soul a hands-on experience that allows it to grow. How does that work? How do they come back to earth in a new body? Did they pick their new life on earth? Does the soul already know the outcome of their life before living it? These are all good questions.

As we start learning what Spirit can do and how things work, I believe this is a good starting point. Here, they start to answer these questions.

> *Intentions of a new life on earth are set by Spirit. The higher self knows all, as it is starting a new earth life and continuing its journey of growth. The soul does select a life*

lesson that will benefit their or someone else's growth. Spirit does know the kind of life situation they will be put in. Not down to a tee, but to the point of free will choices. ★blrd

We have learned, in this book, that they are always around us and hear us from the other side. Spirit is pure love and light. How do they know where to be when needed or called upon? The next message gives us good insight on this very question.

We can see and locate those whose light shines bright. They stand out. Those at peace are recognized by us. Their light energy is like a lighthouse. We can see where on earth this light is missing and we can then work light energy into that area.

Guardian Angels are sent to redirect the light of a soul if it is headed in the wrong direction. This is done only when necessary and their vision of the light is clouded. ★blrd

If the souls of our loved ones can see and hear us all the time, then why don't they give us signs constantly? If they love us and still want to be with us, then why don't they show it more often using signs and communication? These are good questions, that I believe, they have answered very well.

We have complete awareness and knowledge of what you are doing. We cannot control your free will but can intercede at those God moments. We do not give you signs every day of the year. A lot of times to just say hello, and at other times when they are needed.

We know when the time is right. We do not control you with signs. They are simply calling cards of love. ★blrd

Our loved ones do not give us signs constantly for a reason. They cannot be with us all the time and constantly guide our journey. If they did, they would not be allowing for our free will choices to be made. This is our life to live, not our loved ones from the other side. They are here to help in our lives, not live them.

Spirit has said that they know and are aware when their guidance or help is needed. They have said that they can pick up on our vibration. They say that they can intercede at those God moments without changing our free will. How does this work?

> *Angels, Guardian Angels, and souls do intervene. They can do it using vibration, by themselves, or by using someone else to do what is needed. They use people that will get your attention. Like using an attractive woman to get a man's attention. Something that stands out or grabs the attention of the person needing guidance. Spirit uses little nudges to redirect us when needed.* ★Gandolf

> *Divine intervention is when things are made right. It is a correction. It is when the free will of many has set things into motion and a correction needs to be made. This happens when something the person needs to do in this life is not finished or started. This can be a lifesaving event, a change in course, or even an afterlife experience.*

> *This happens when the highest beings of light need to step in and make the correction. It truly is divine intervention. It is made to happen by those of the highest light. This happens with the high energy like Jesus used. It is of the highest order and nature.* ★blrd

Time is different on the other side. It does not exist like it does here on earth. Time, like religion, is man-made. This is done to keep things in order. On the other side, everything is done with love and for the greater good of all. I can attest to time not existing there, due to my afterlife experience. In this next message, they try to explain how time is different there.

> *"It happened in the blink of an eye." That is how time works on the other side. You can video something here on the earth plane and hit pause at any point when watching it.*
>
> *Next, you can expand that image with your fingers. But instead of expanding in, expand out. Now you have an image of countless things that happened in that instant.*
>
> *So, you have captured a lot more than you thought was possible. That is how time works on the other side. Limitless things can be comprehended in the same instant. This is an example of how Spirit can communicate with multiple people at the same time, who are in different places.*
>
> *Time and space are different on the other side. They can be here too. We just need to learn how to capture our time/space, expand it, and go into it.* *blrd

Wrapping up this subject of time not existing on the other side like it does on earth, I want to mention a few more things that I was given. This also gives an example of how Spirit travels and gets to where they need to be. I love the following message I received.

> *Everything here is infinite, vast, and immense. The speed of light (love) exists. Time and speed are love. When you want to go somewhere, there is no effort used to get there, just thought. Travel and speed are simply thought. Therefore, time is meaningless.*
>
> *We do not think of things in terms of time or time allotment. We think of things as love. A peace that we keep growing and building upon.* *David

As we continue to learn about how things work on the other side, I want to share this quick lesson on love. I have mentioned the word love countless times in this book. I have done so because it is the answer to everything. It is peace. Love cures all.

> *Love on the other side pulsates. It is an energy that is pure. This pureness is pure love and light. The same kind of pureness associated with Jesus. This pureness is absolute. It is the beginning and the end. It is all. It is everywhere and everything. It is God.*
>
> *This absolute pureness of love and light is an energy that overcomes all. It is final. It is all that is. The compassion and understanding that comes with it is the overwhelming love and light of God, the Source. All answers and truth are found in this absoluteness.* *blrd

I want to share what Spirit taught me about how the higher self exists on the other side. I found this information to be mind-blowing. I had never heard this or even really thought about it. This next learning lesson given to us shows how everything really is connected in this one consciousness. There truly is no separation. I am still blown away by this message, months after it was given to me.

> *Your higher self is already enjoying its time with your loved ones on the other side. That is why when you are connecting to loved ones in your sleep, you are seeing the part of this relationship that is ongoing. There is no separation. This goes to show just how unimportant your body is in the whole scope of things.*
>
> *At cross over, there will be an awakening. This awakening will give instant memory of what the higher self has experienced. This will include experiences we had*

with our loved ones on the other side, as our higher self, while living in our bodies here on earth.

Our lives on earth keep us from being aware of all that is going on in the no separation and one consciousness of all that is. There is still a reunification at a soul's cross over. It is more like an understanding and awakening. There is still a life review.

*Everything here is temporary. It truly is a school of souls learning lessons on earth. The higher self, lives in eternity, the body does not. This is another reason your loved ones are so happy on the other side. It is because there is no separation. *blrd*

Continuing with this, I wrote this in my journal after receiving this wonderful information. *That is how it works. Loved ones on the other side get to experience things with my higher self. My higher self gives me a connection to them. This is how signs and things are given at times. The higher self helps in this process just like guides do.*

Wow! That is a lot of information to take in and digest. This previous message may be one of the most profound and eye opening I have ever received. It really does change my perspective on how I view everything and all that is.

Finishing out this chapter, I want to briefly write about what Spirit gave me about exit points. These are points in our earth life that are our predetermined time to go. A part of our reincarnation trip that was set into motion with our new earth life. There may be many possible exit points in our life. When one of these occur, it may not be the right time. Something may not be finished that we came here to do or learn.

I want to share a brief story to put into context their message about exit points, since the message was directed to me. When I was a teenager around the age of seventeen, I went on a vacation with my parents and sibling that was still living at home. We were in our car on the interstate driving through Florida.

As I sat in the backseat of the car behind my dad, who was driving, a semi-trailer tire, rim and all, came bouncing past my window. It could not have missed our car and my window by no more than twelve inches. It was a spare tire from the trailer of a semi-truck that had rattled loose and started bouncing down the crowded interstate. Unbelievably, it bounced around and ended up in the median of the highway without hitting anything or anyone. I could not believe it.

I have never forgotten that close call. Like other times in my life when there were close calls, it just was not the right time for my exit point. I still had work and learning to do here on earth. Was this the divine intervention that we just talked about? Here is what Spirit says about this in the following short message.

> *Exit points in life on earth do exist. For you, possible exit points include the semi-tire incident, the electric cord story, the almost being crushed by the car scenario, and others. These exit points existed, but it was not what was in your life plan. It was not your time yet. You still had work to do. When your work is complete, your number will be called.* ★Lida

Summing up this chapter, we have learned how new souls are created. We have learned about souls planning earth life journeys and how they can locate us. Spirit has told us about how they can intervene from their place of timelessness. They have told us that we have a reason to be here and we do not use our exit point until that task has been realized.

The most intriguing lesson, I believe, in this chapter is about how the higher self has already reunited with our loved ones on the other side. We catch glimpses of this ongoing life of ours in our dreams. We have never really had any separation.

A lot of people live in the fear of the unknown. They may not be able to heal and grow spiritually because some remedies, to these fears, are different than what society has taught us to believe. We have the fear of being, or going it, alone.

If you take nothing else with you from this chapter, take this wonderful message from Spirit with you. That message is that we are never alone! There is never any separation! We are always connected to everything and everyone through love! This love is absolute, pure, and the beginning and end of all that is. It is final. Love is the answer to answer all questions.

CHAPTER ELEVEN

● ● ●

What Do Souls Living on the Other Side Do?

IN THIS LAST chapter, we will simply let Spirit tell us about some of the things they do in their everyday lives. Most people who have lost loved ones, at some point, have questions about this very point. Since there is an afterlife, then they should still have a life to live. They cannot spend eternity floating around the universe unintentionally with no purpose.

As I said earlier, the other side is simply another world of existence. Their vibration, on the other side, is much higher than ours. This keeps most people from seeing souls here on earth. It is like we co-exist. They seem to be in a different dimension than us. This dimension though, does allow for them to live a life.

Most of the time, in this chapter, I will tell what Spirit has told me instead of quoting them. They have taught me so much about the other side in the last couple of years. It has been an honor.

The lives they live in their dimension, on the other side, are about learning and growing as a soul. They have places of higher learning, just as we do here. They also can relax and enjoy this wonderful place of love.

Souls are not hardcore driven to be the best or better. They are at one with *all that is*. They understand from their peace that all is as it is supposed to be. In my morning connection this morning, they just so happened to briefly speak about this very subject.

> *Once you have found your peace, you no longer need to prove anything, be better, or stronger. You simply are. This simple knowing allows you to understand your true essence. Being at peace gives you success at all that is.* ★blrd

Again, Spirit has plenty of time for rest and relaxation. They love to have hobbies and goof off just like we do here on earth. This is an important lesson that Lida once gave me. He let me know that they like to have fun too. There are times when he does not do anything but play around when I am with him. This is his way of letting me know not to take myself too seriously.

As a soul, you are free to go and learn and grow as you please. Of course, there will be counseling sessions spent with one or more of your guides. They will help advise and guide you in the right direction. They are still a part of your journey and there to assist.

Every soul has its own personal journey. The soul understands this. As a soul, there is nothing but accepting what is best for the greater good of all.

On the other side, the soul grows, learns, heals, and gets

to be with loved ones. They then can come back for another carnation trip of learning lessons on earth. The soul understands what it needs to experience and learn on its next earth trip. It also knows and understands when it is ready to come back.

My son, David, has told me that you can do anything you like there. You can hike, fish, go to parks and stadiums full of people. If you are an artist, then you can do artwork. They also have houses and villages. You are free to do as you choose to do. You can continue education and listen to lectures and speeches. There are no limits.

David goes on to tell me that they can visit us here anytime. If someone is needing comfort or healing in a hospital, they may be called upon to assist. This is part of their soul growth. They have the ability and freedom to move around in the love and light of God like being on a superhighway. The speed limit though, is the speed of love and light.

Spirit tells me that there are villages of learning. Each village has its own unique area of growth. There are small groups of souls, like clusters, that vibrate at the same levels. Together they learn in these specific subjects and areas. They resonate with each other and have the same needs. A lot of these villages have buildings that look like temples.

These villages are on the outskirts of the City of Light. The City of Light is where the beings of the highest light reside, along with the palace of light. Lots of holy work and spiritual development are done in these two areas.

You can also continue to practice religion. It may be altered somewhat from when you were here on earth, but it is common practice. These practices can only be done if they resonate in the White Light. Anything that does not resonate in the White Light has a vibration that is too low to function properly there.

Things kind of work in this sequence-

Cross over/ White Light- angels, love, and family.

Palace of Light- love, angels, and a life review.

City of Light/ Villages- love, temples, learning, and growth.

Working and growing in soul groups.

Soul groups are bonding times. A time to work with other similar souls. In them there is unity, love, and helping each other. This is a time when the soul has freedom to roam, help people here, communicate and give signs. It is a bonding and friendship time. It is time of renewal and love.

Most of our family is in our soul group. They may vibrate differently, so we may not be with them all the time on the other side. We can be with them whenever we want. You are with your family at this point, but you have your own thing to do. It is a time of freedom. A time of working on things to raise your vibration and draw nearer to oneness with the light.

Everything flows in unison on the other side. There is an understanding and knowing. These qualities give souls balance in all they do. All souls have the same common goal. This goal is making themselves and everything and everyone else better with love for the greater good of all.

Make no mistake about it, if you have a loved one on the other side, they are having the time of their life. Time is different there, so the time that you *think* you are separated from them is only the blink of an eye on the other side.

They are living in a world of having a free heart like a child again. They have no worries. Souls are healed from whatever ailed them while living on earth. Your loved one is walking in a balanced world of freedom which gives them peace. They have gone home.

Their soul will make connections with you through your higher self. Anytime you feel as if a loved one is visiting you it is because they are. This visitation can be in the form of a dream.

Listen with your heart. Live your own journey. Never let anyone discourage you. You are you. You are important. You matter.

Do not let someone else's truth of you be your truth. Go deep and find your own truth (peace). It is there. Stay the course. Stay true to yourself. Allow others to use their own free will. Do not get in the way of another finding their peace and you will find yours.

Your higher awareness lies in the space connecting both worlds together. There, time is no longer relevant, and 'I' takes on a plural meaning. This is where your peace on earth is found within. Here, you are home and realize the meaning of pure love and acceptance.

One might think that God did not create all these differences amongst people. People are unique. Why would he do that? When it comes down to it, God did create all these differences in people. This is because everyone is God. Everyone is a part of the unseparated one consciousness of God.

All the differences in people are a good example of how everyone is on their own personal journey. We could not learn lessons, here on earth, if everyone were exactly alike. There would be no differences between us to learn from. Others are teaching us lessons through our differences. That is the beauty of it all.

Always remember, love is the answer to answer all questions. You will find this love within. Look no further. You have the answer inside you right now.

As I move forward on my own personal journey, Spirit has been showing me something new. Sometimes it takes me several connections to start flowing and understanding what they are trying to teach me. That is how it works for me. A new lesson starts with a seed planted by Spirit that may take some time to develop and grow.

In my new lesson, Spirit has been showing me a large staircase. It is made of fine wood and is about seven feet wide. This staircase is approximately twenty-two steps tall and near the top it curves to the left. At the top is a place of higher vibration and love.

As I recently journaled about this staircase during my morning connection, Spirit told me that the staircase leads to a *hall of records*. In this area of records, I have been given access to all that has been, what is, and what will be. It is a place that I can go to and access information.

Spirit then gave me the word *biometrics*. I wrote it down in my journal during that morning connection. I did not have a clue of what the word meant. I wrote it down because I accepted what Spirit gave me, even though I did not understand it.

A couple of days went by and I had forgotten about the word *biometrics*. I just happened to hear it used in conversation, so I searched for its meaning on my phone. I just could not believe what I read.

I immediately went into my spirit room to get my journal. I found the page where I had written the word *biometrics* in my connection earlier that week. It was right under what I wrote about Spirit giving me access to information in the hall of records.

Biometrics is a way to identify you biologically to give you access to a specific area. It is like when you put your finger on your smart phone to unlock it. Using this biometric method of access gives someone entry to, and unlocks, where they need to go.

I understood right away what Spirit was trying to tell me. They were telling me that I was being given entry and access to all the information in the hall of records. They were saying that my vibration was now aligned with the vibration at the top of the steps. This alignment was now giving me biometrical entry into the hall of records. How cool is that?!

Spirit knows that I will follow up on, and research, what they give me if I do not understand it. This is called *trusting Spirit*. Let them guide you and they will lead you to where you are meant to be.

After learning this lesson from Spirit, I put it to use in my next connection. I, along with Lida, Reece, and David (blrd), went into the hall of records. It is kind of like a library. There are volumes of books on shelves that seemed to go on infinitely. There are also tables there to sit down at and use.

I sat down at one of the tables after pulling a black bound book off one of the shelves. I opened it up and a lesson started playing out in front of me like those of a holographic nature. Here I was, sitting with *blrd* in the hall of records, starting this new part of my journey. I was amazed at what I saw and was learning! It was fascinating and simply unbelievable!

In this lesson, Spirit started teaching me about.......

Wait a minute.
Did you hear that?
I need to go.
There they are, down at the end of the hallway!
I invite you to join me!
Let us do it together because we are never alone!
Free your heart!
Let your emotions run wild!
Throw your hands up in the air!
Do not worry about what others might think!
You are now starting to heal from your loss!
You are living again!
Run like the wind!
Let us do our part!
In **THE KINDERGARTEN RUN!**

Bob Jacobs has also written two other books.

FIFTY YEARS OF SILENCE NO MORE
BECAUSE I HAVE BEEN THERE

Printed in the United States
By Bookmasters